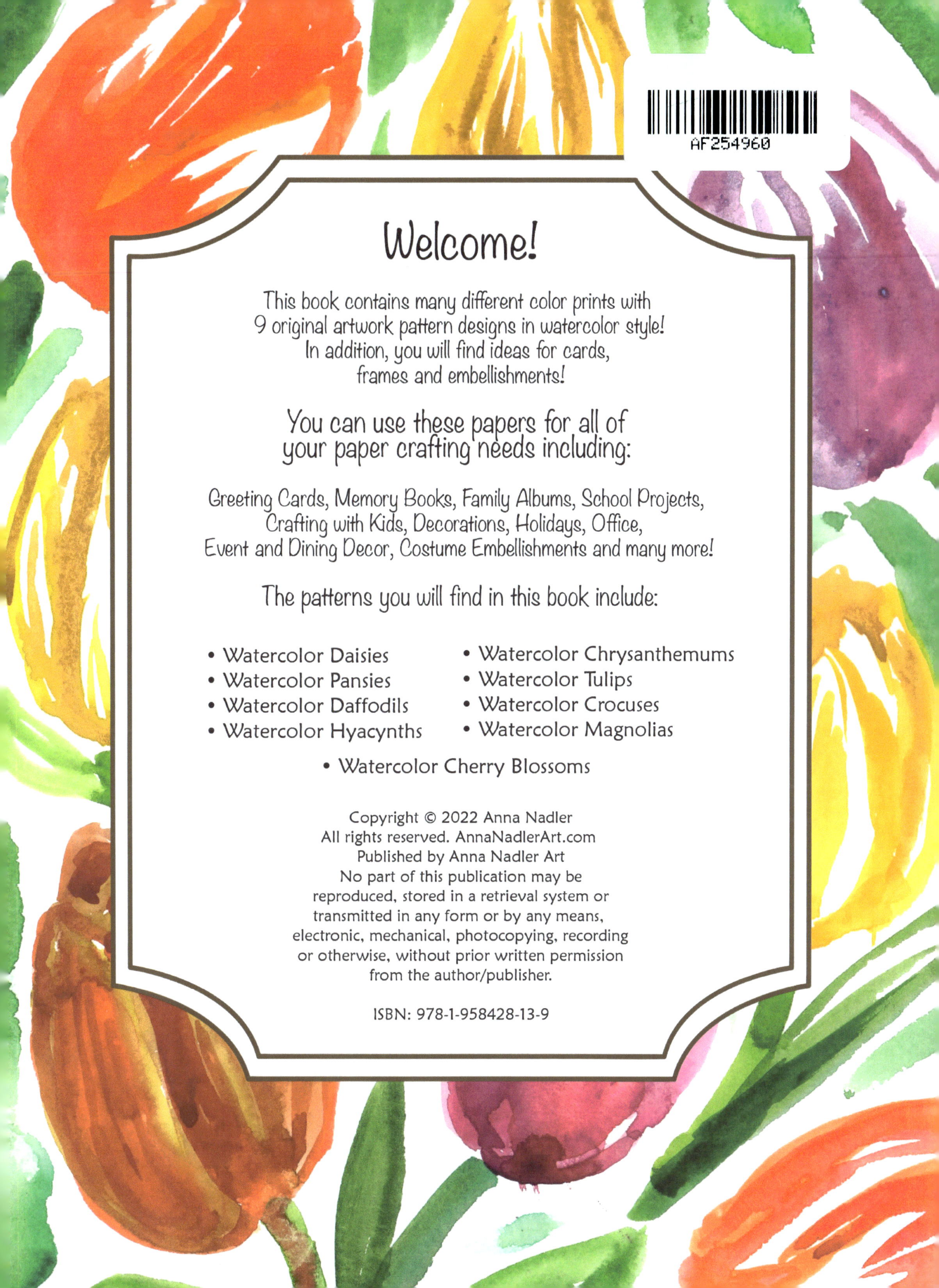

Welcome!

This book contains many different color prints with
9 original artwork pattern designs in watercolor style!
In addition, you will find ideas for cards,
frames and embellishments!

You can use these papers for all of
your paper crafting needs including:

Greeting Cards, Memory Books, Family Albums, School Projects,
Crafting with Kids, Decorations, Holidays, Office,
Event and Dining Decor, Costume Embellishments and many more!

The patterns you will find in this book include:

- Watercolor Daisies
- Watercolor Pansies
- Watercolor Daffodils
- Watercolor Hyacynths
- Watercolor Chrysanthemums
- Watercolor Tulips
- Watercolor Crocuses
- Watercolor Magnolias
- Watercolor Cherry Blossoms

ISBN: 978-1-958428-13-9

Design Ideas

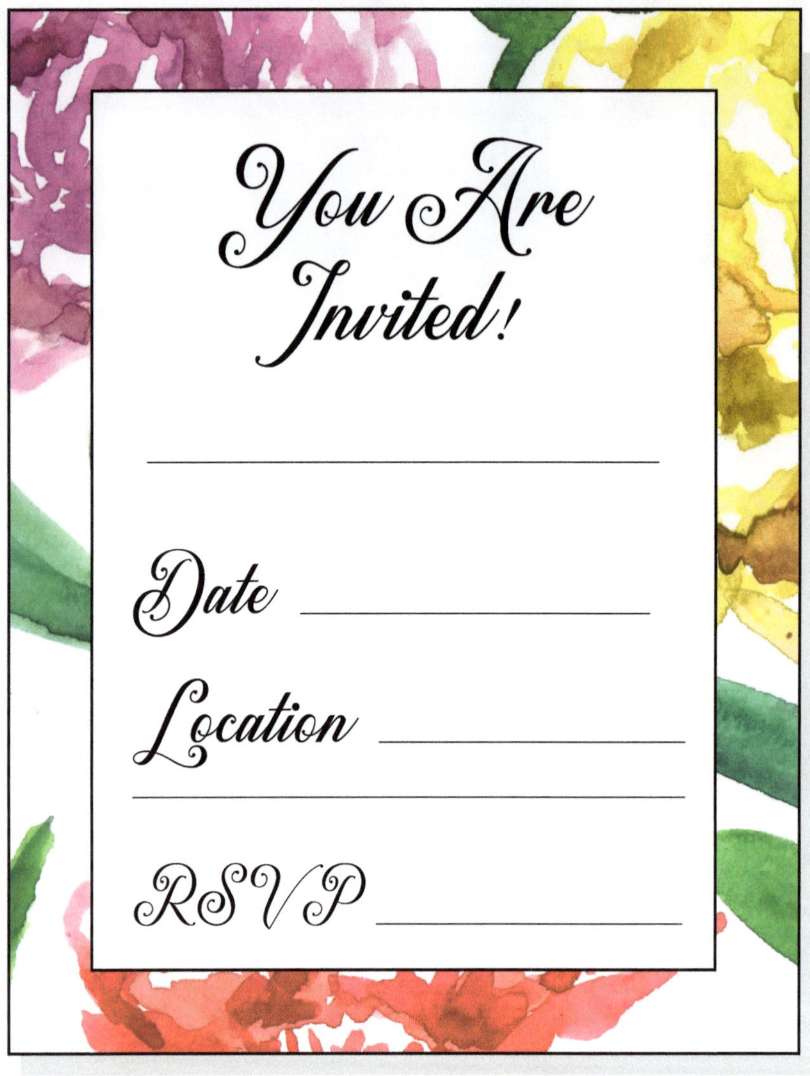

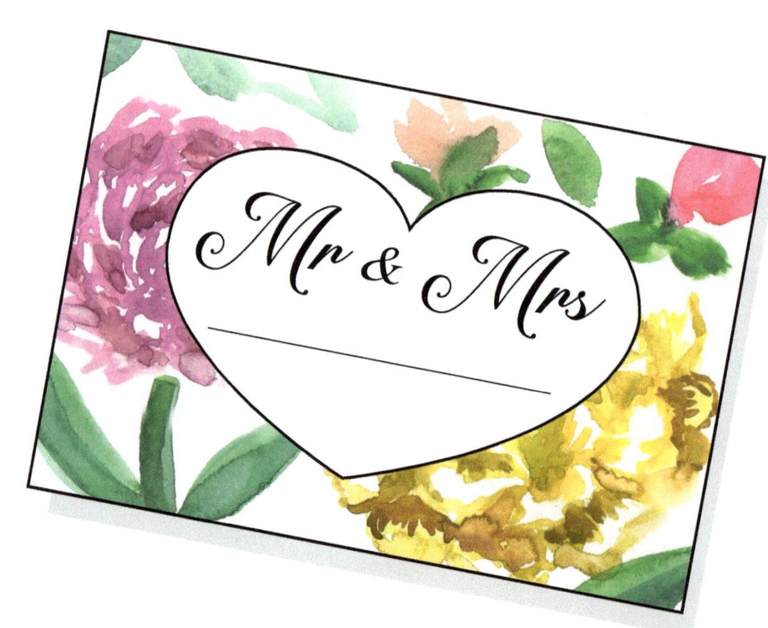

Design Ideas
Happy Birthday!

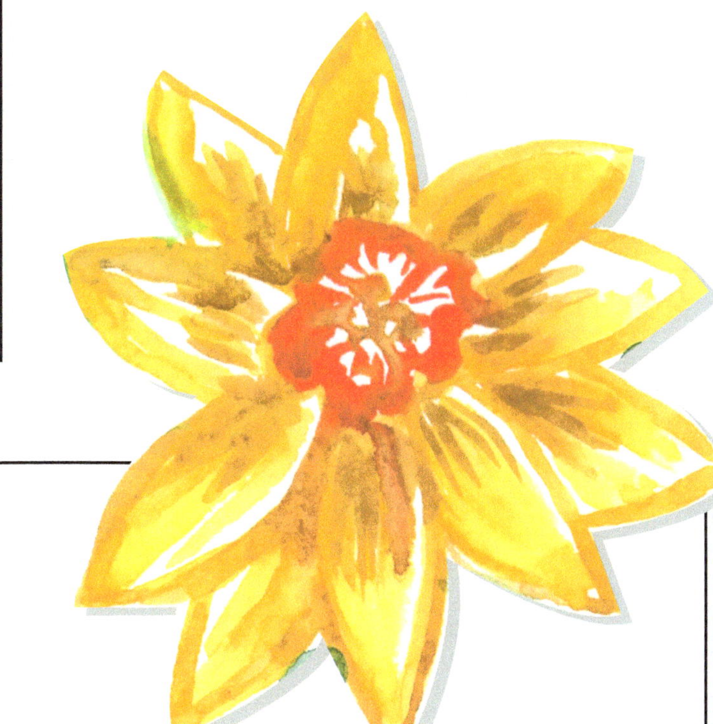

Congratulations!

Frames

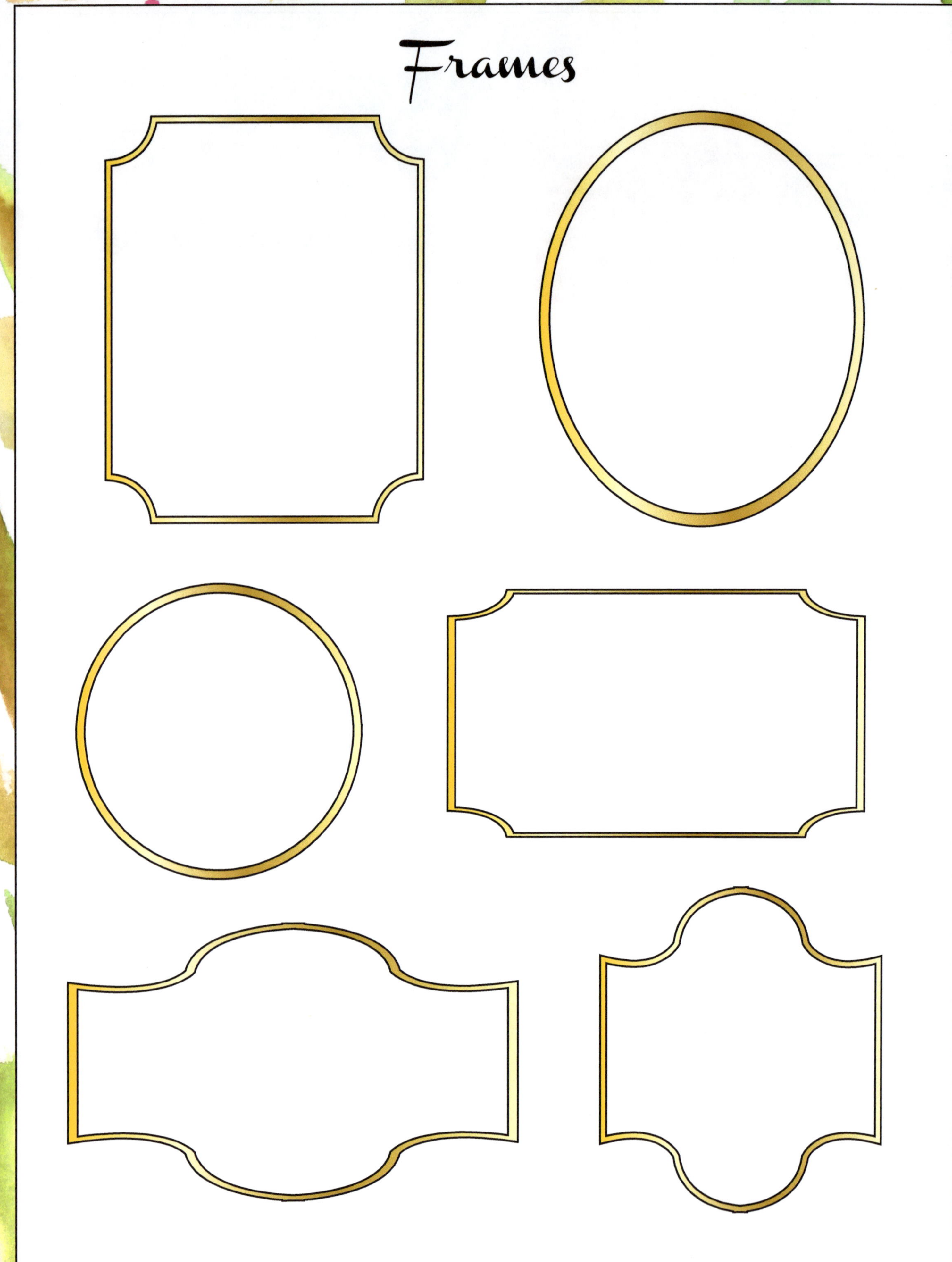

Ribbons

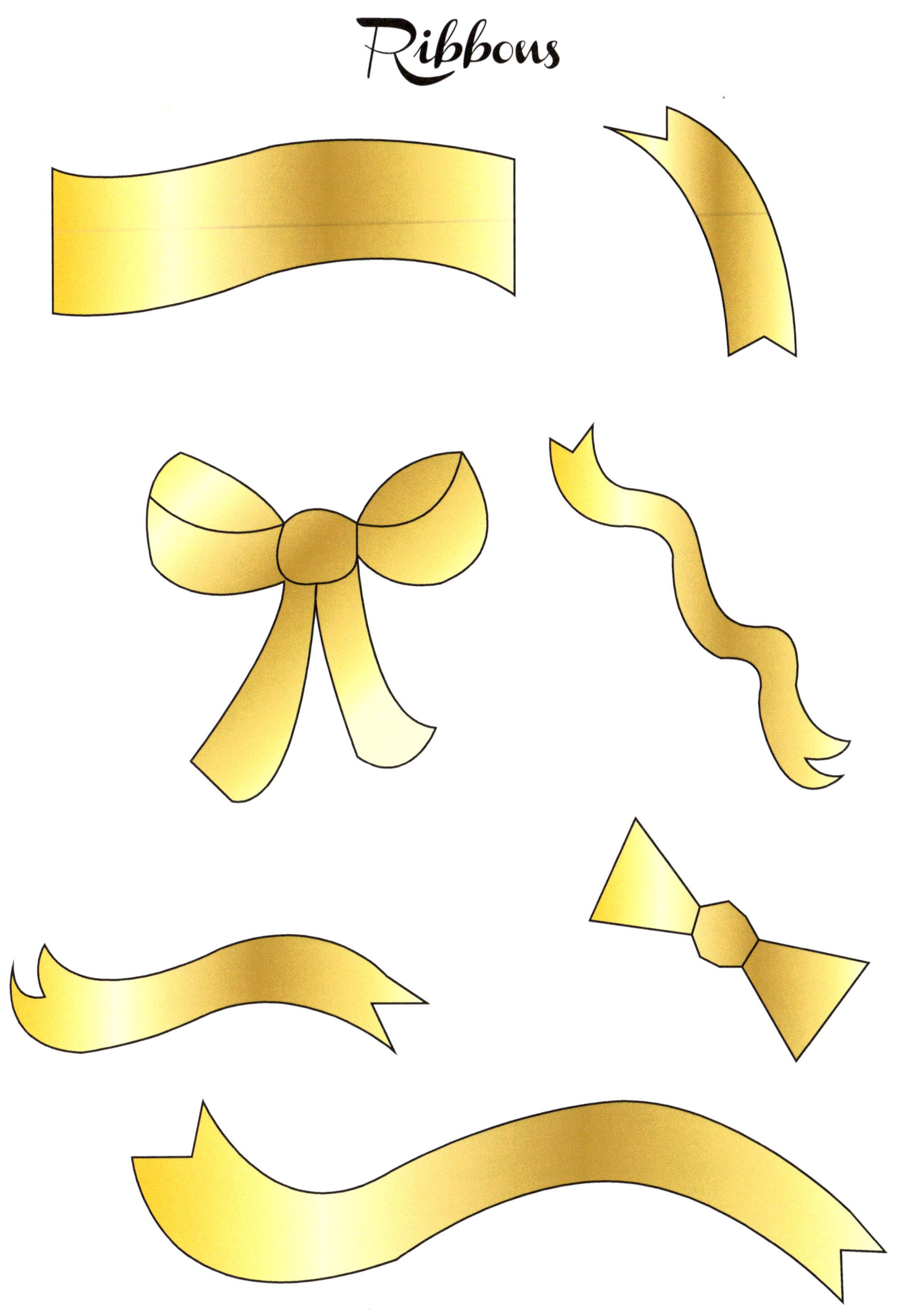

Daffodils

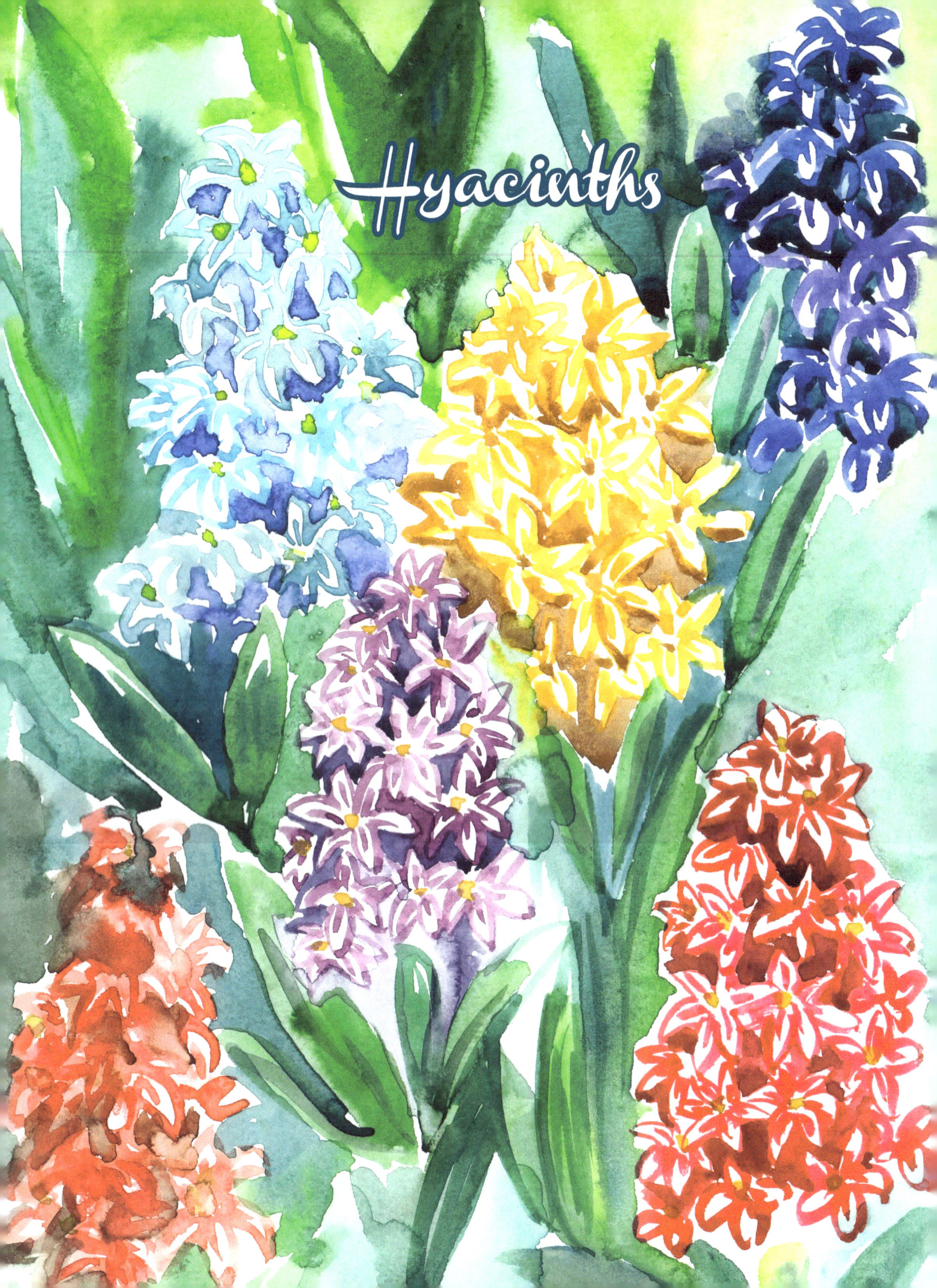
Hyacinths

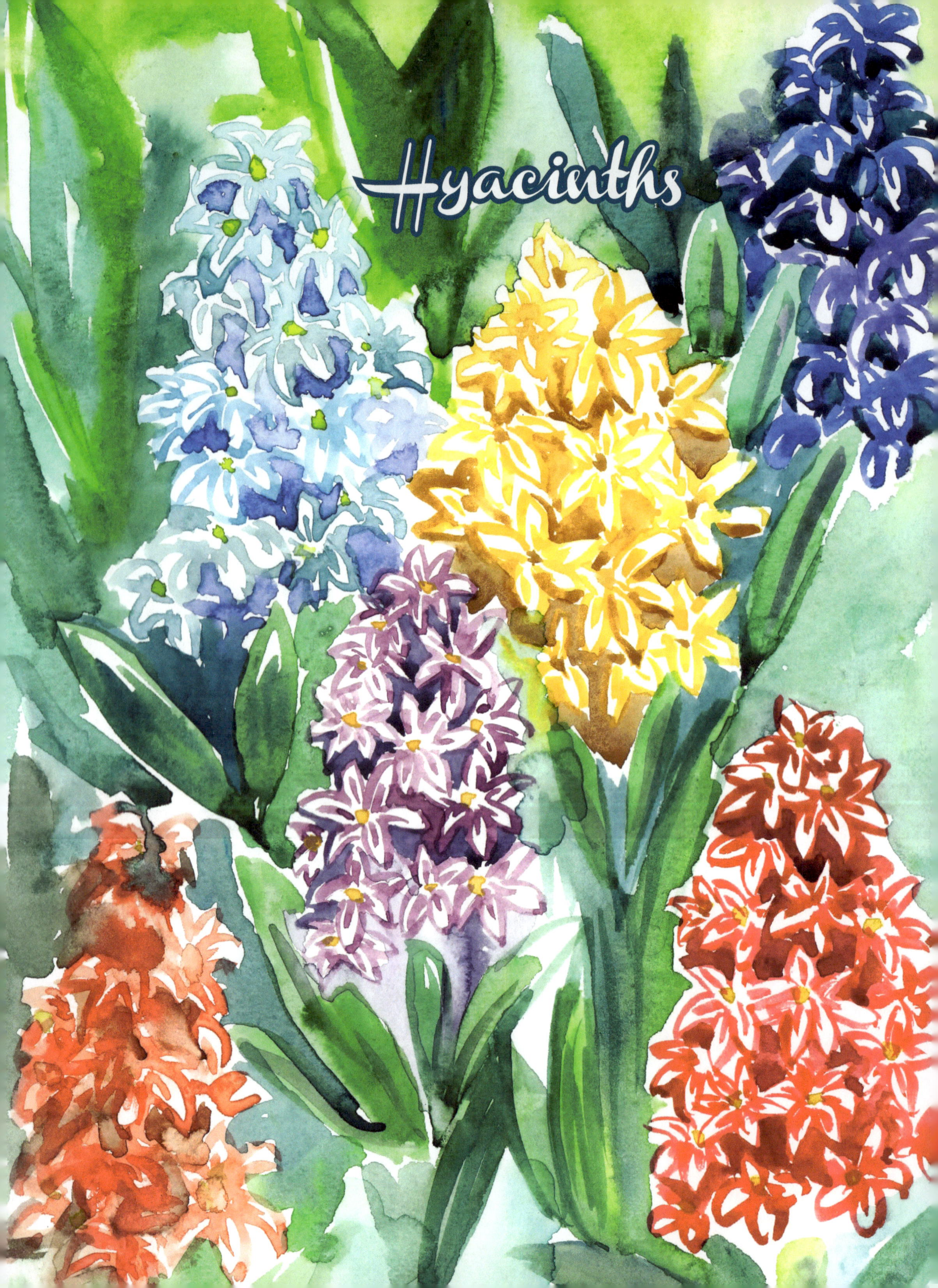
Hyacinths

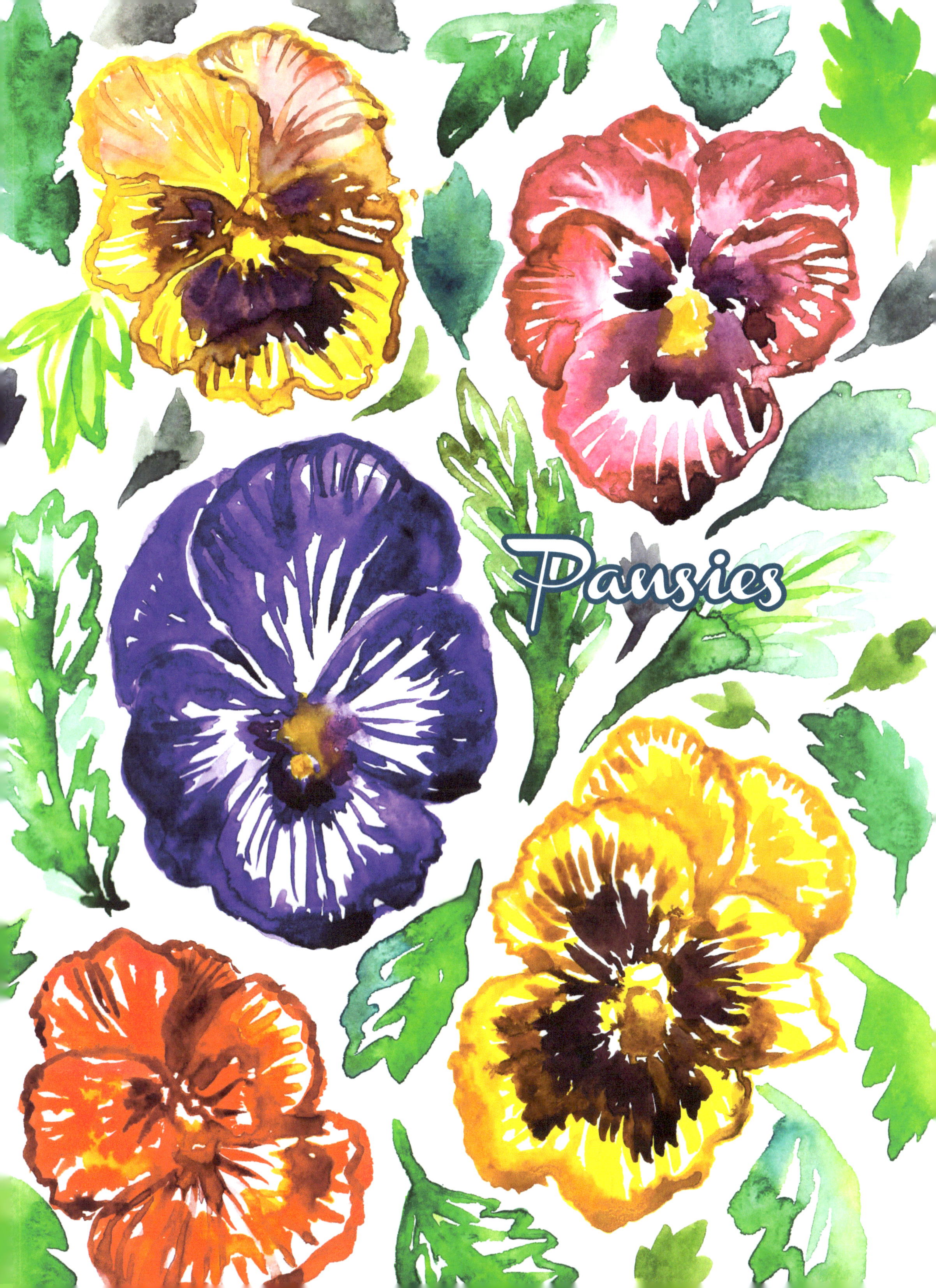
Pansies

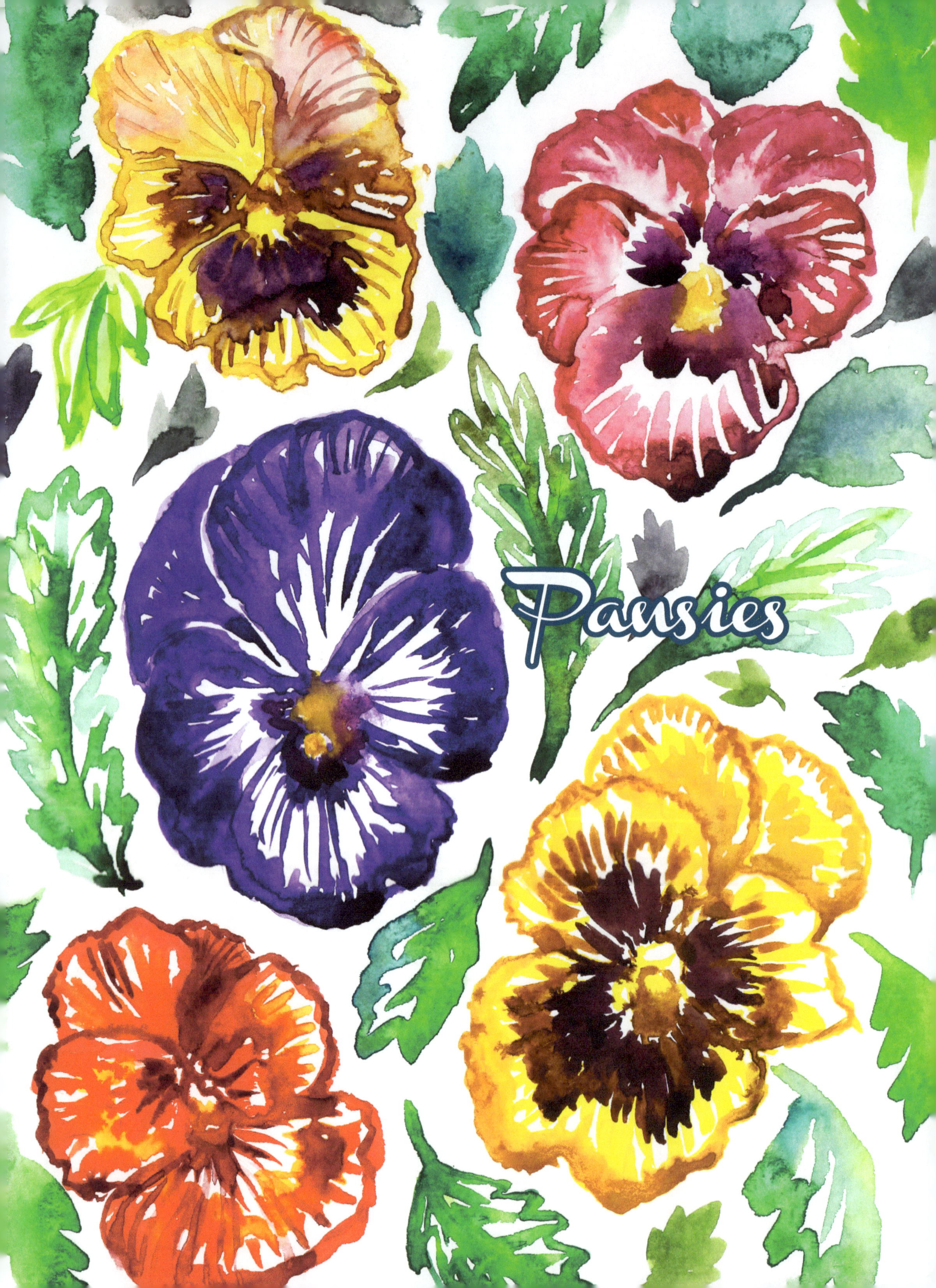
Pansies

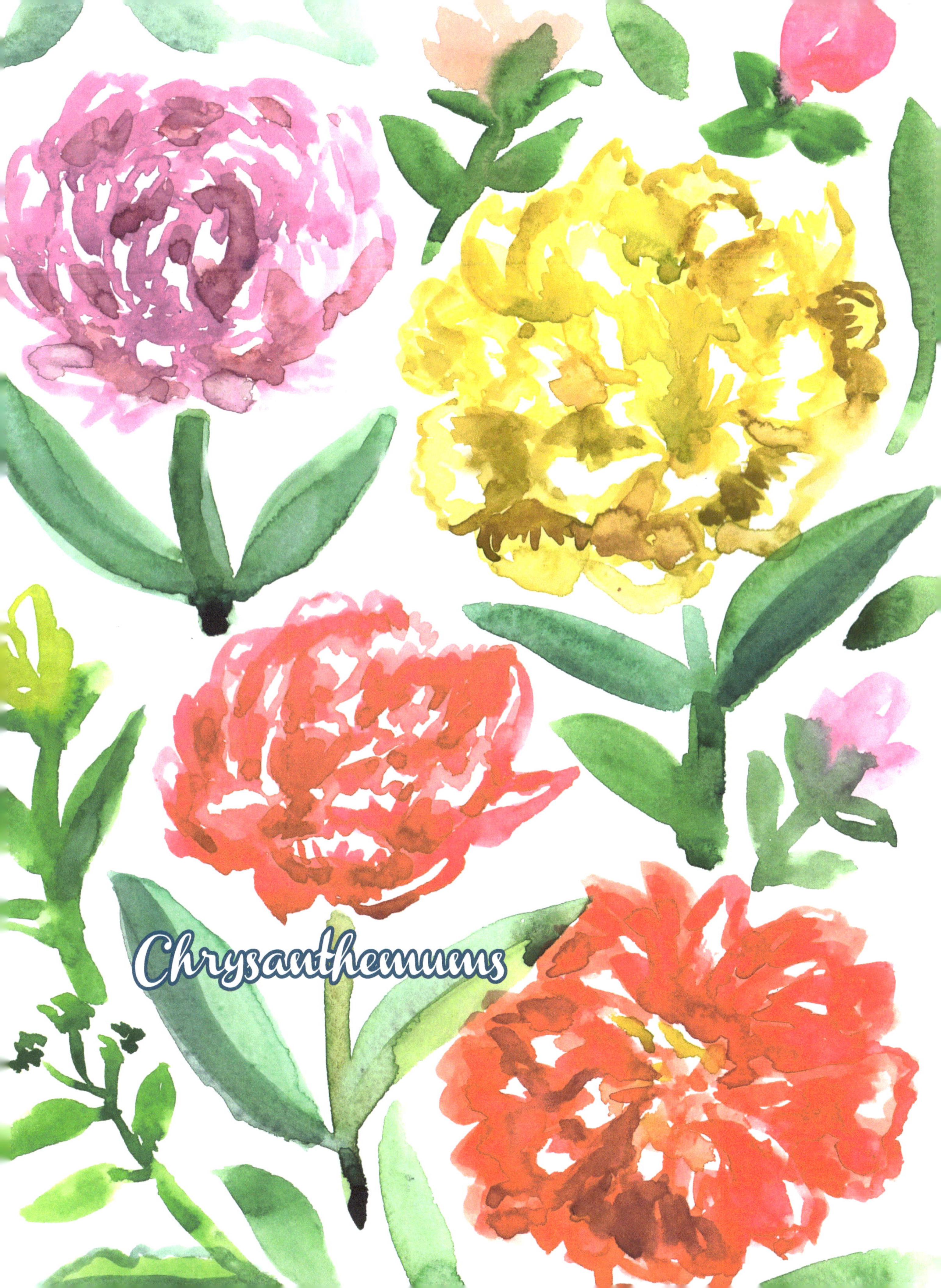
Chrysanthemums

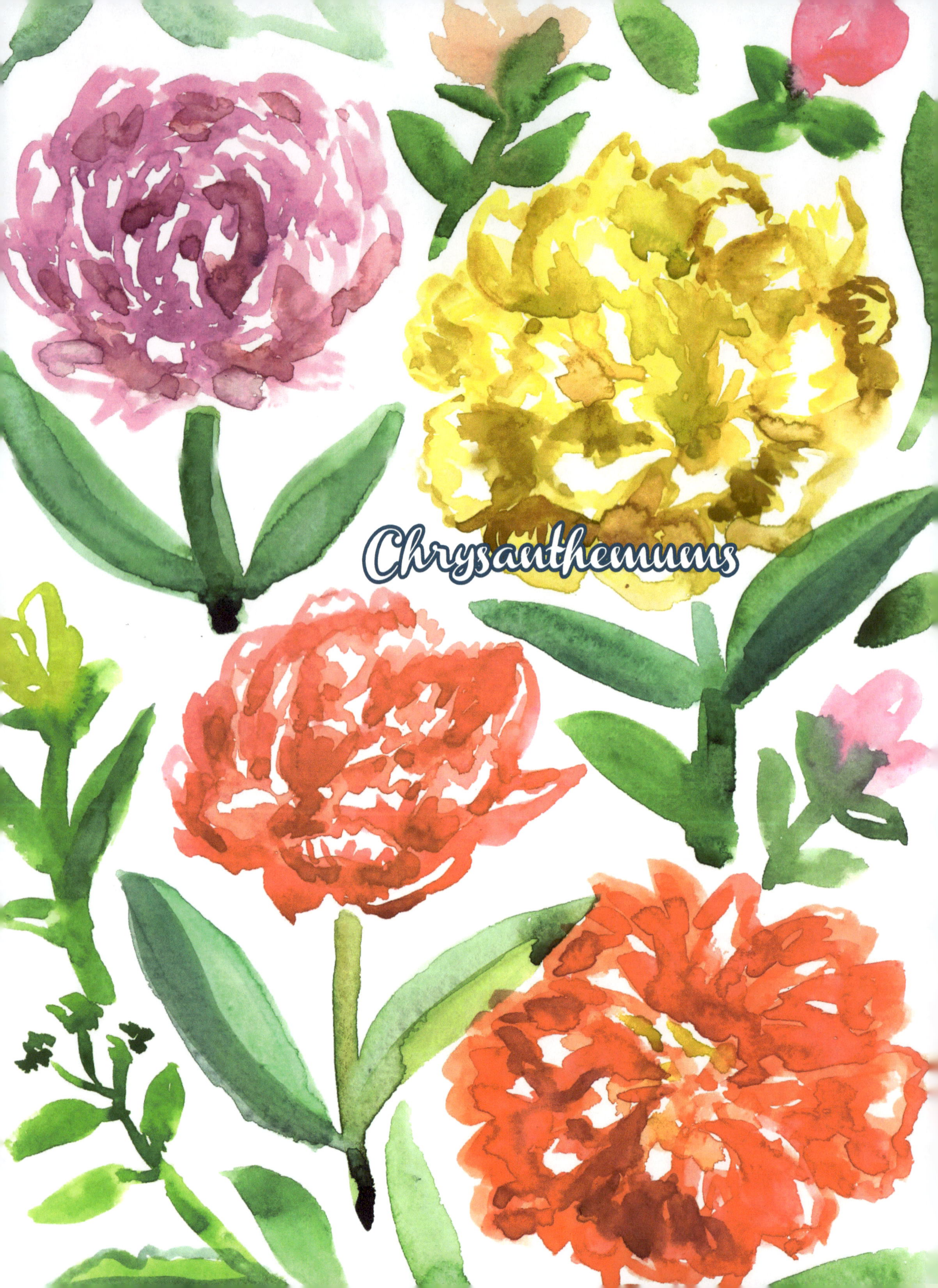

Chrysanthemums

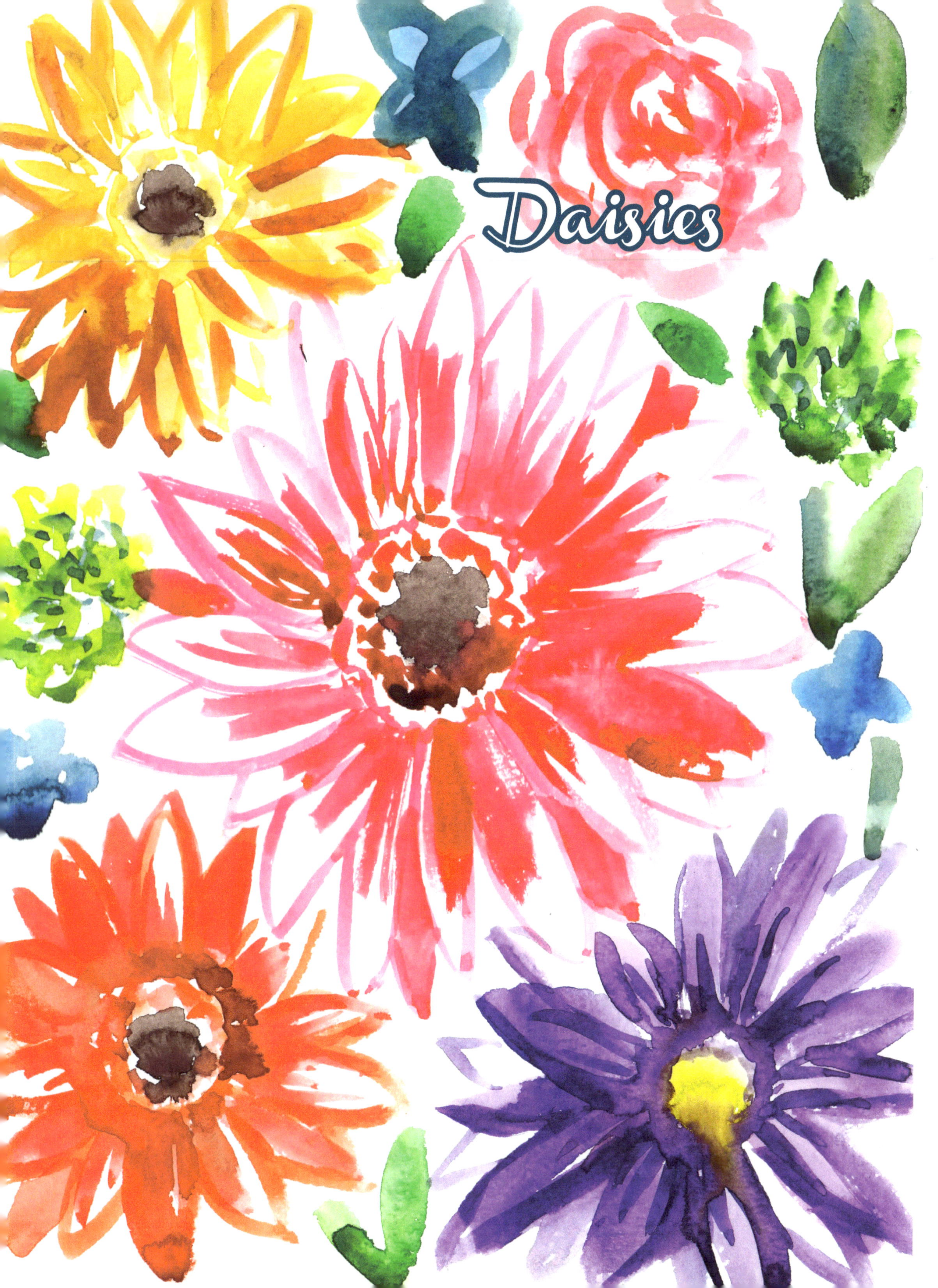
Daisies

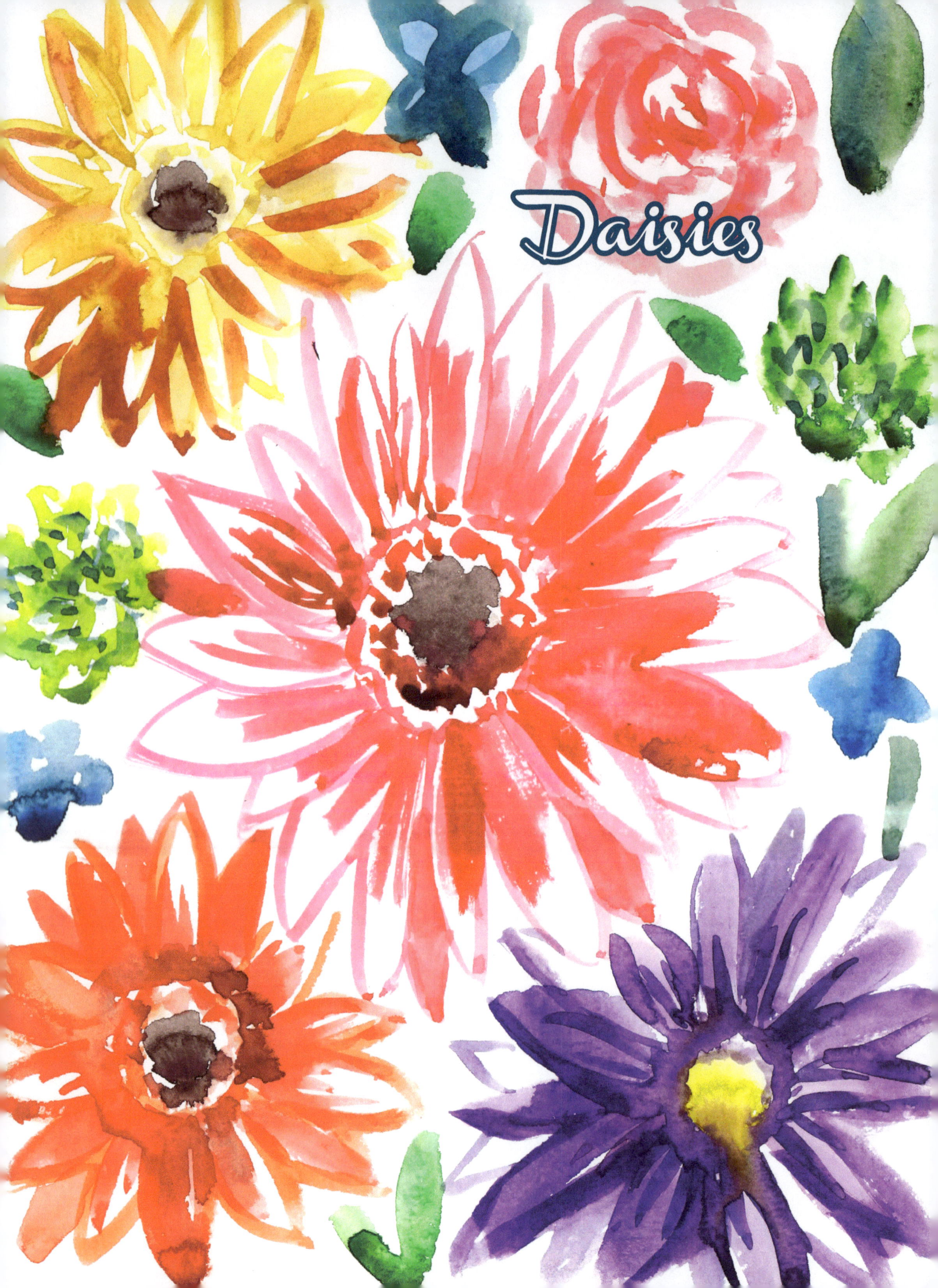
Daisies

Magnolias

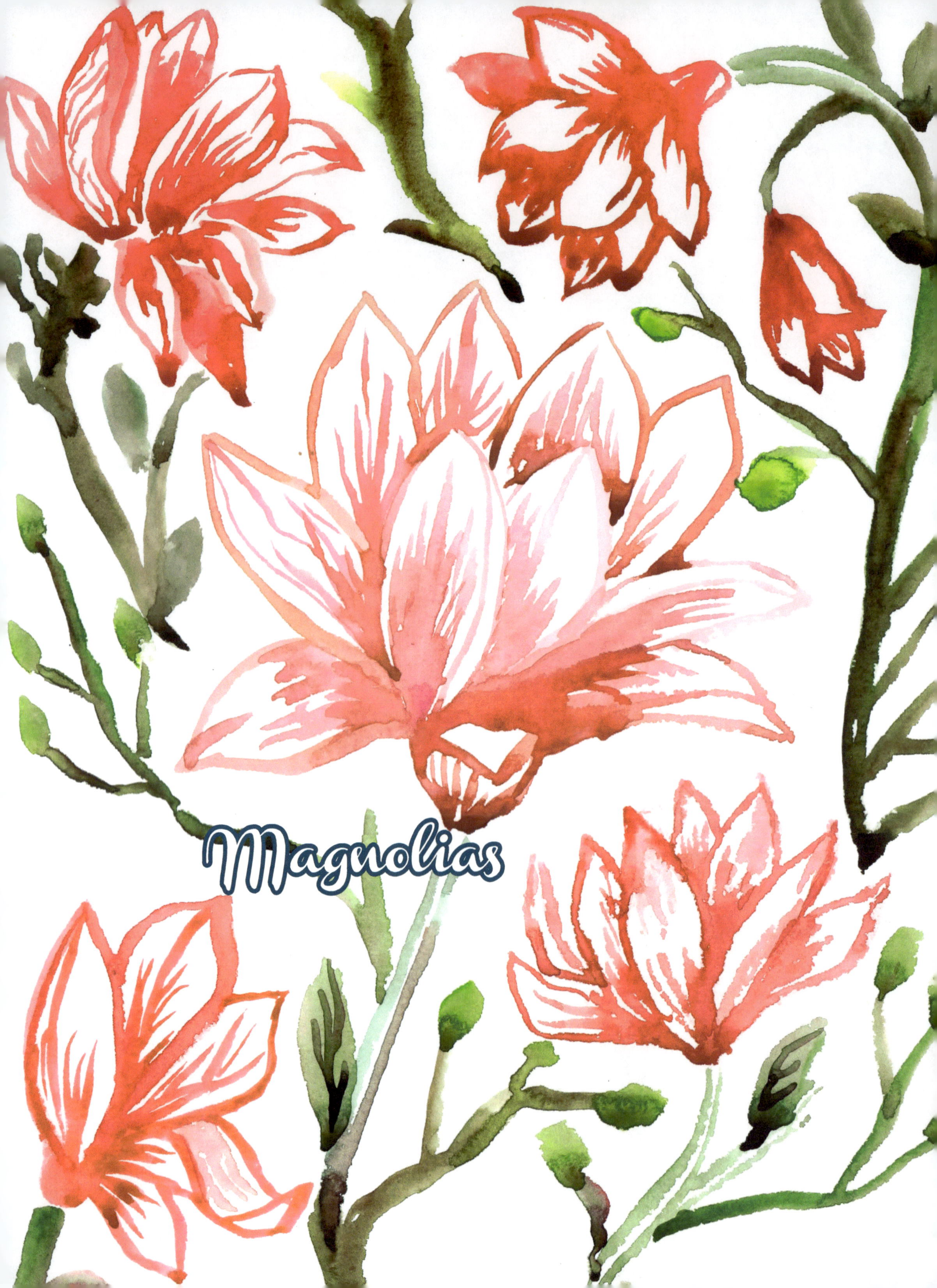Magnolias

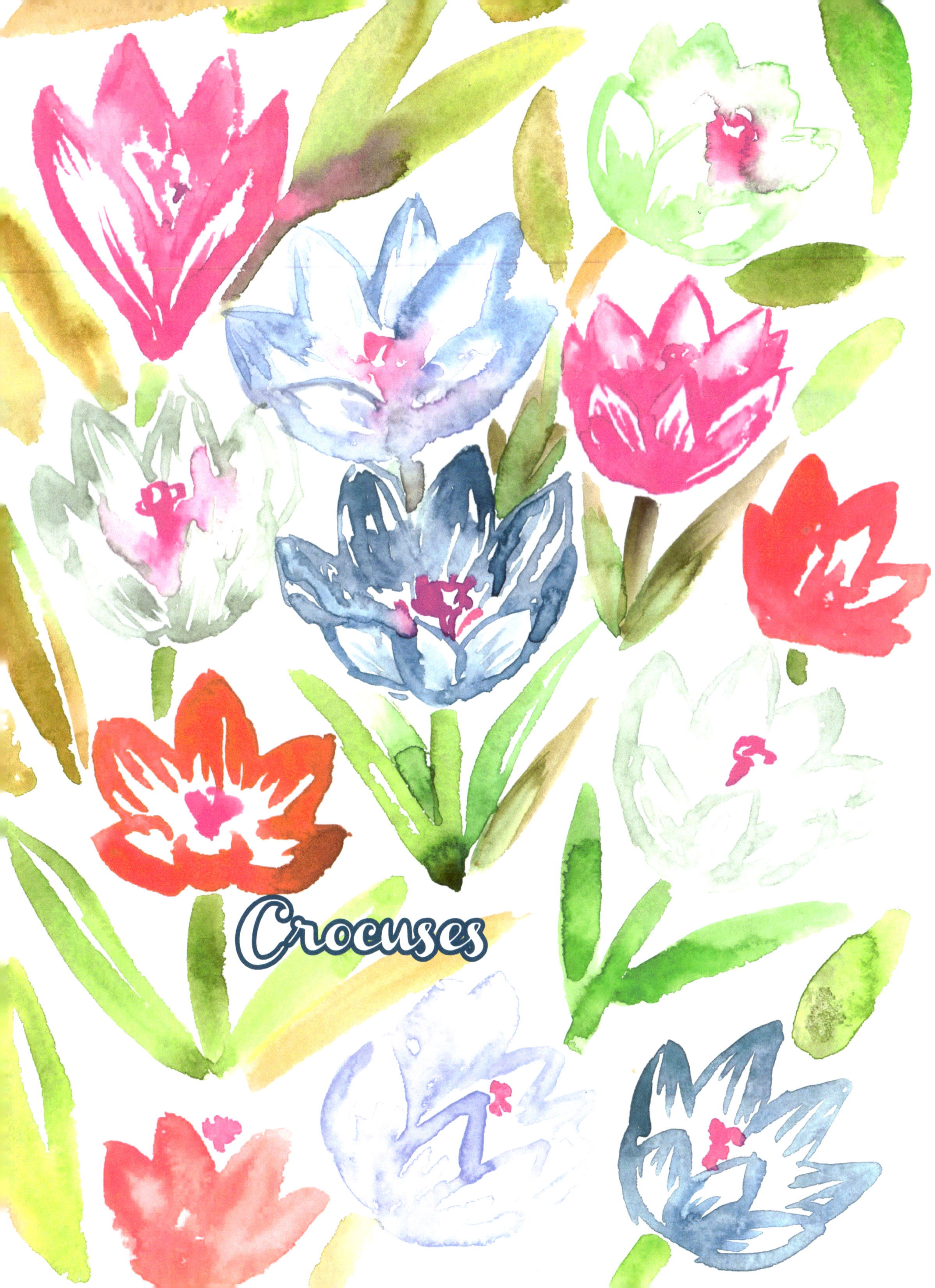

Crocuses

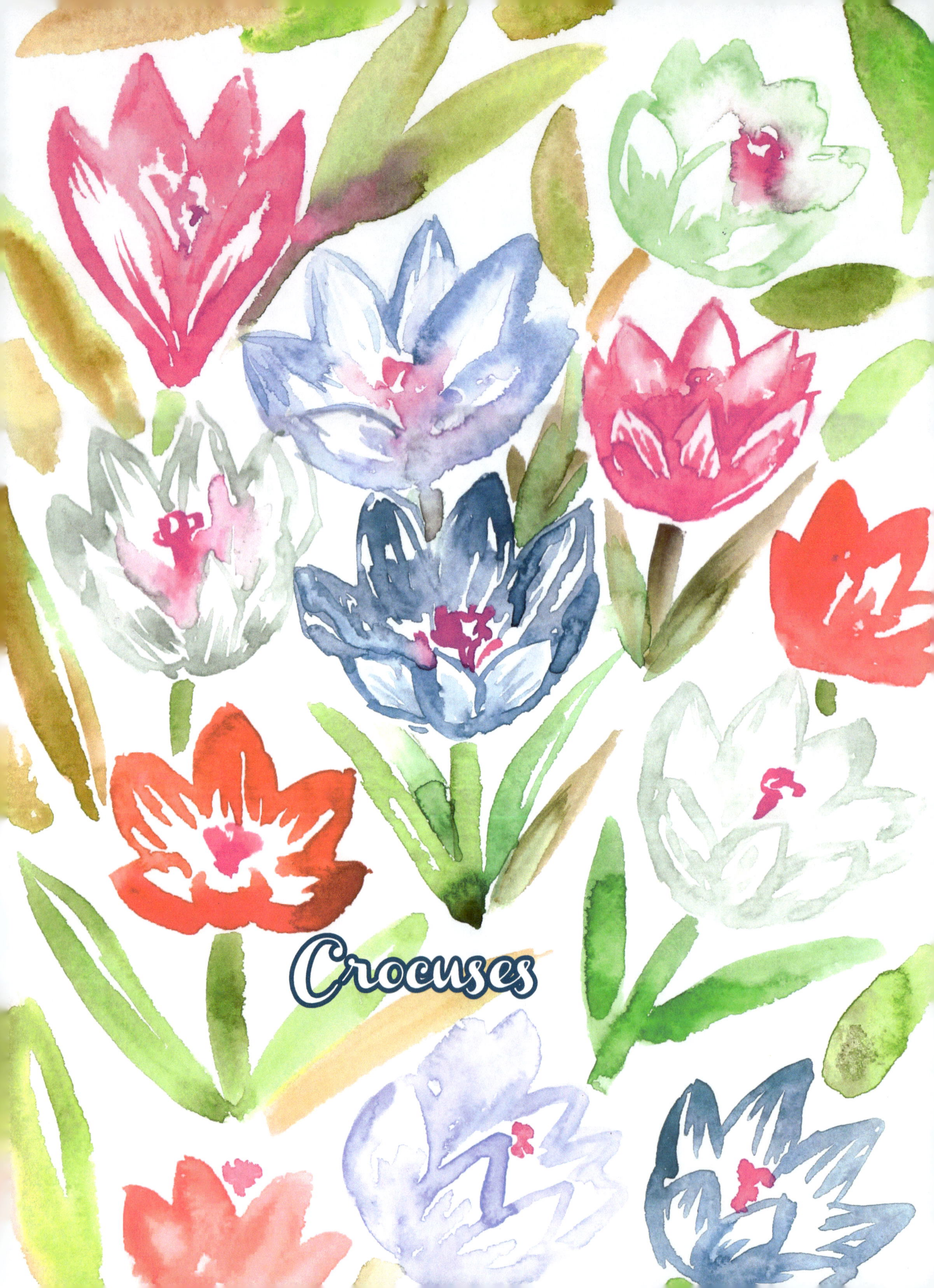

Crocuses

Daffodils

Daffodils

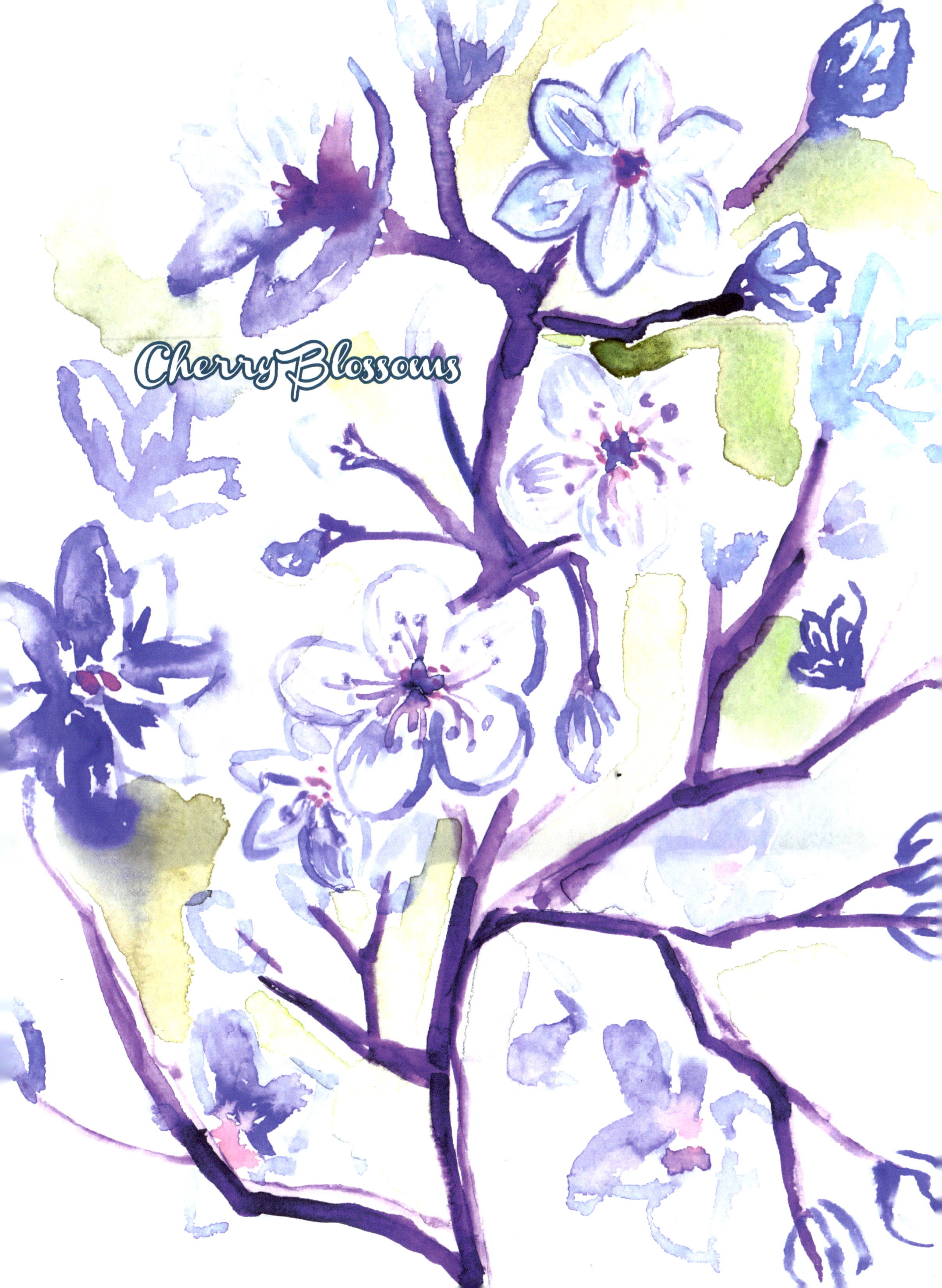

CherryBlossoms

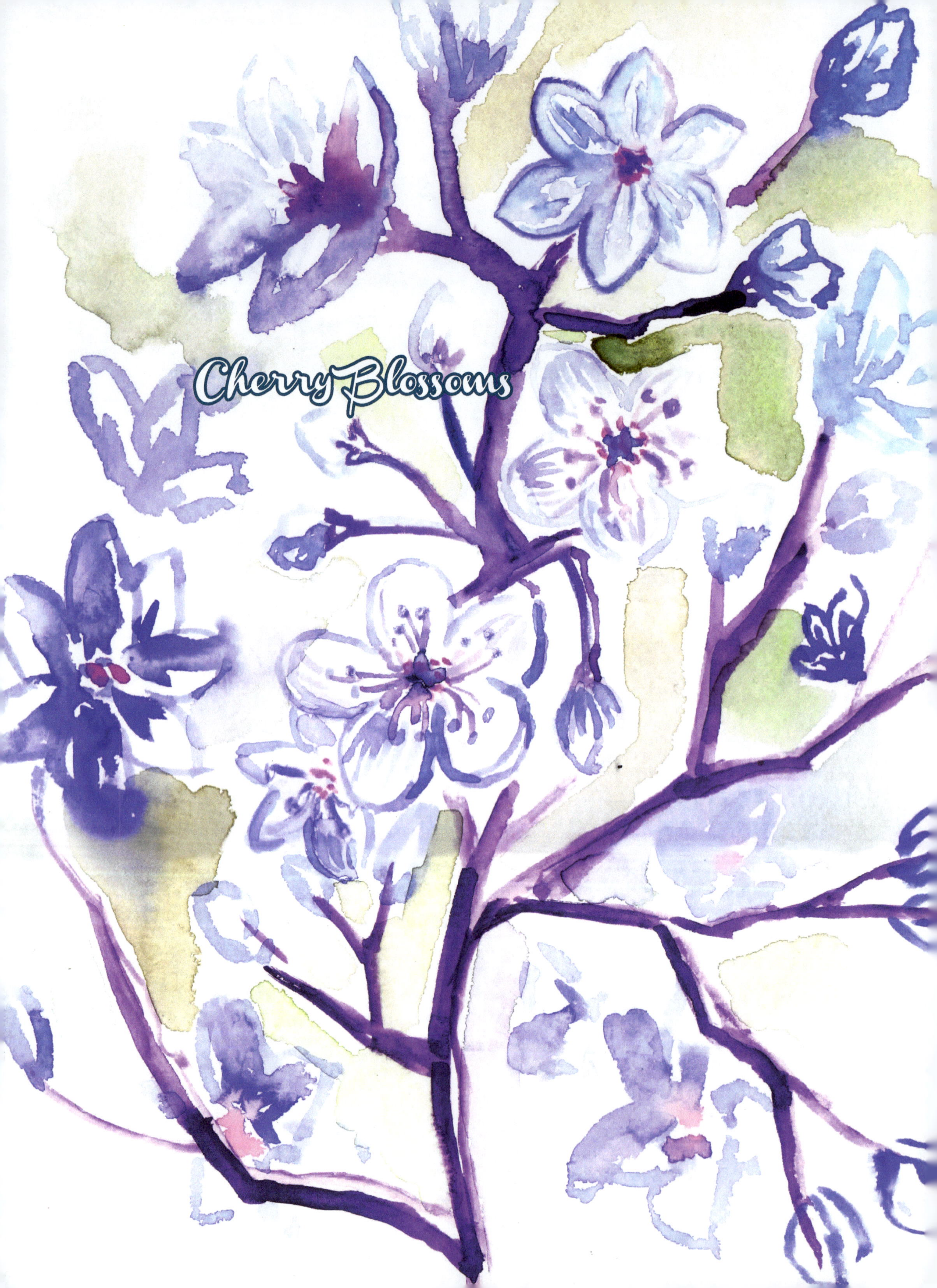

Cherry Blossoms

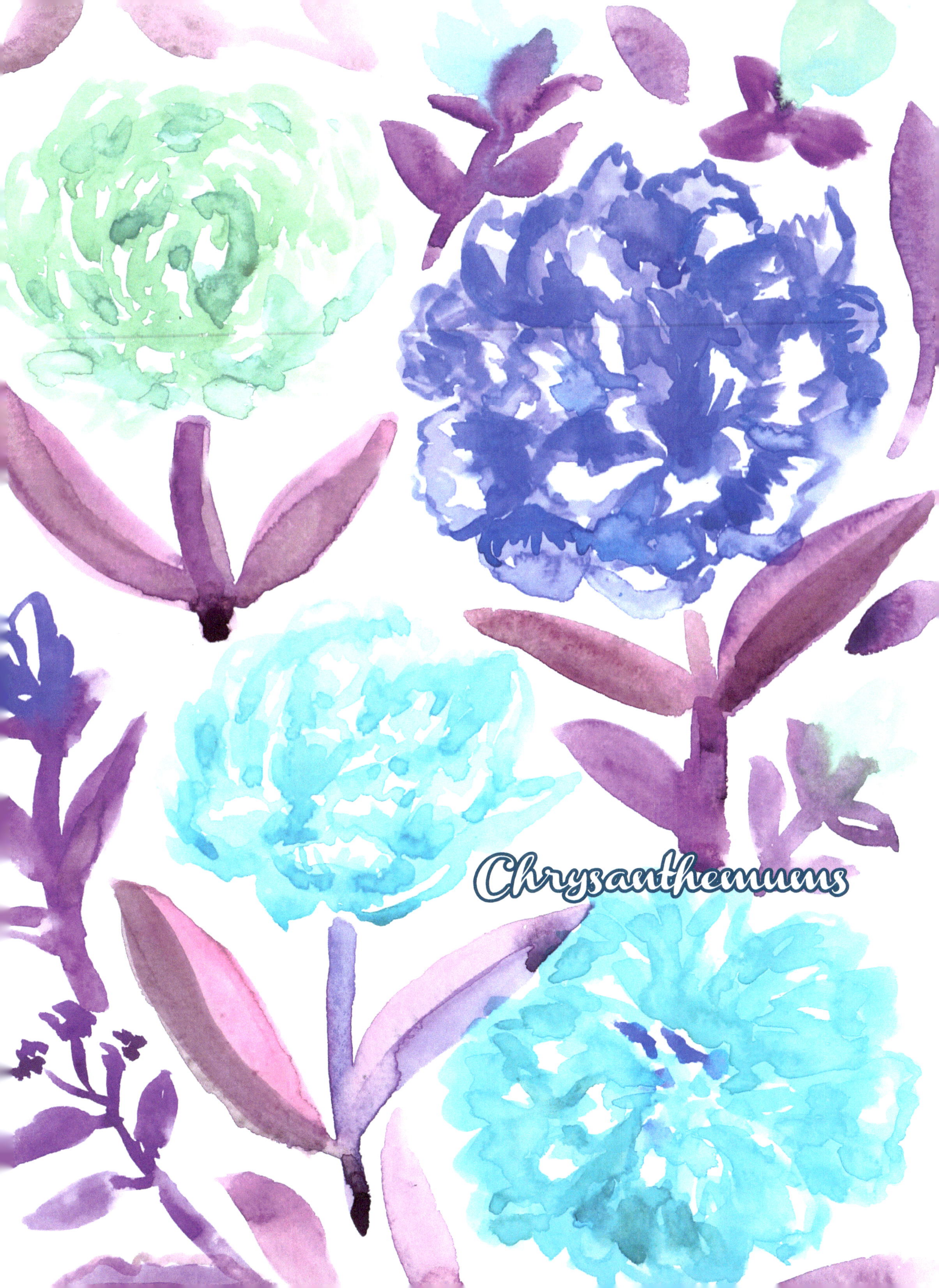
Chrysanthemums

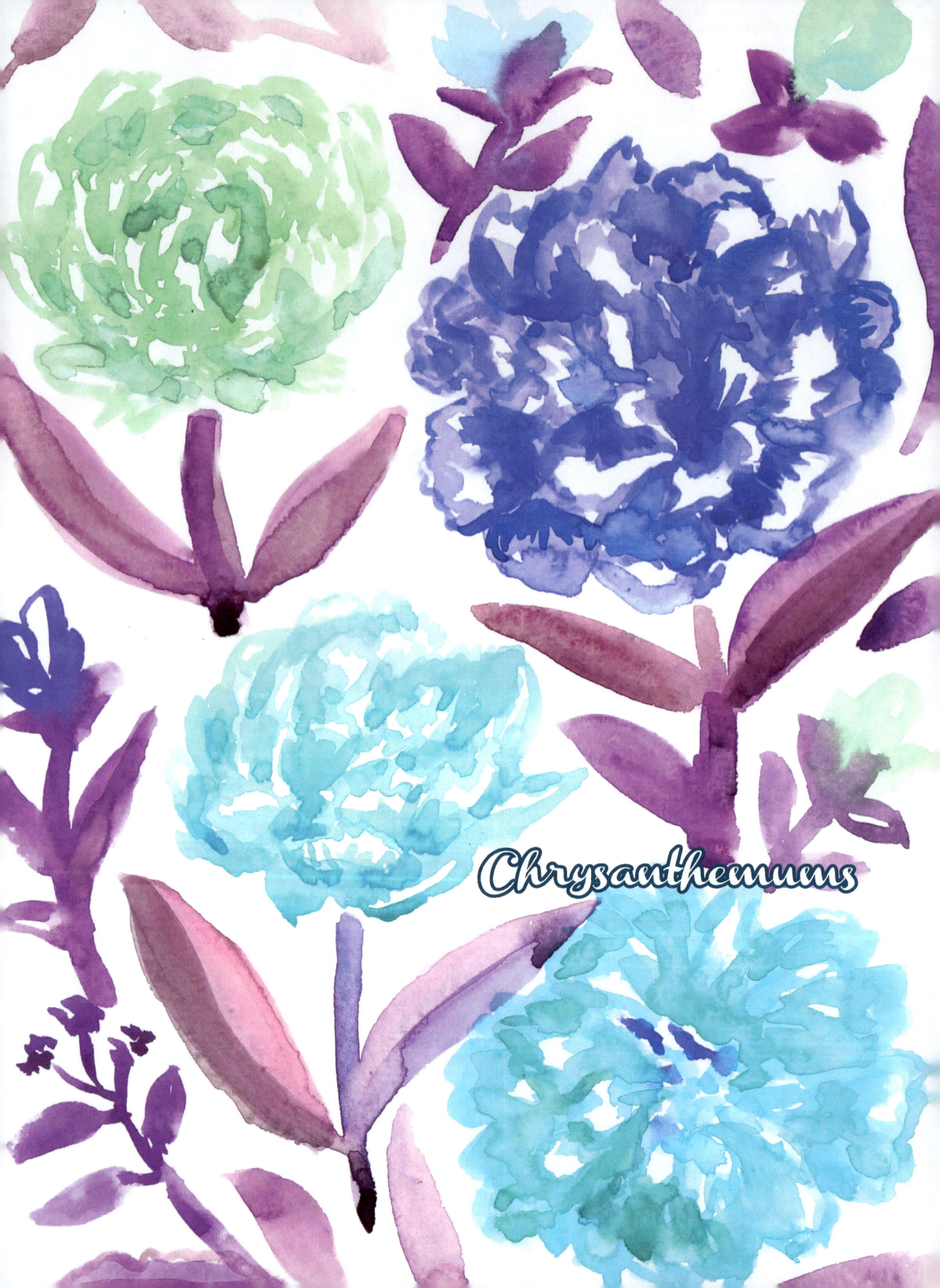
Chrysanthemums

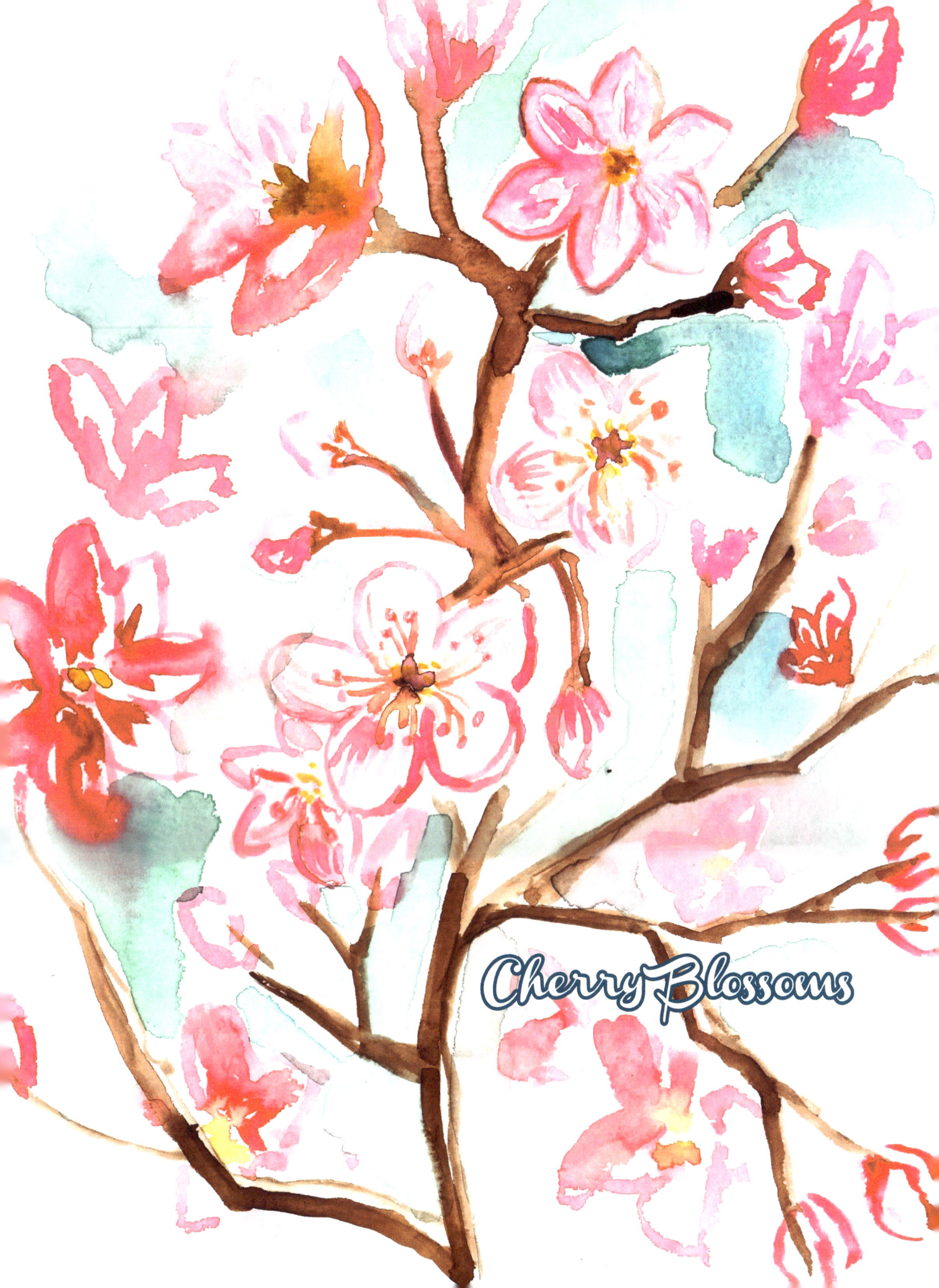
CherryBlossoms

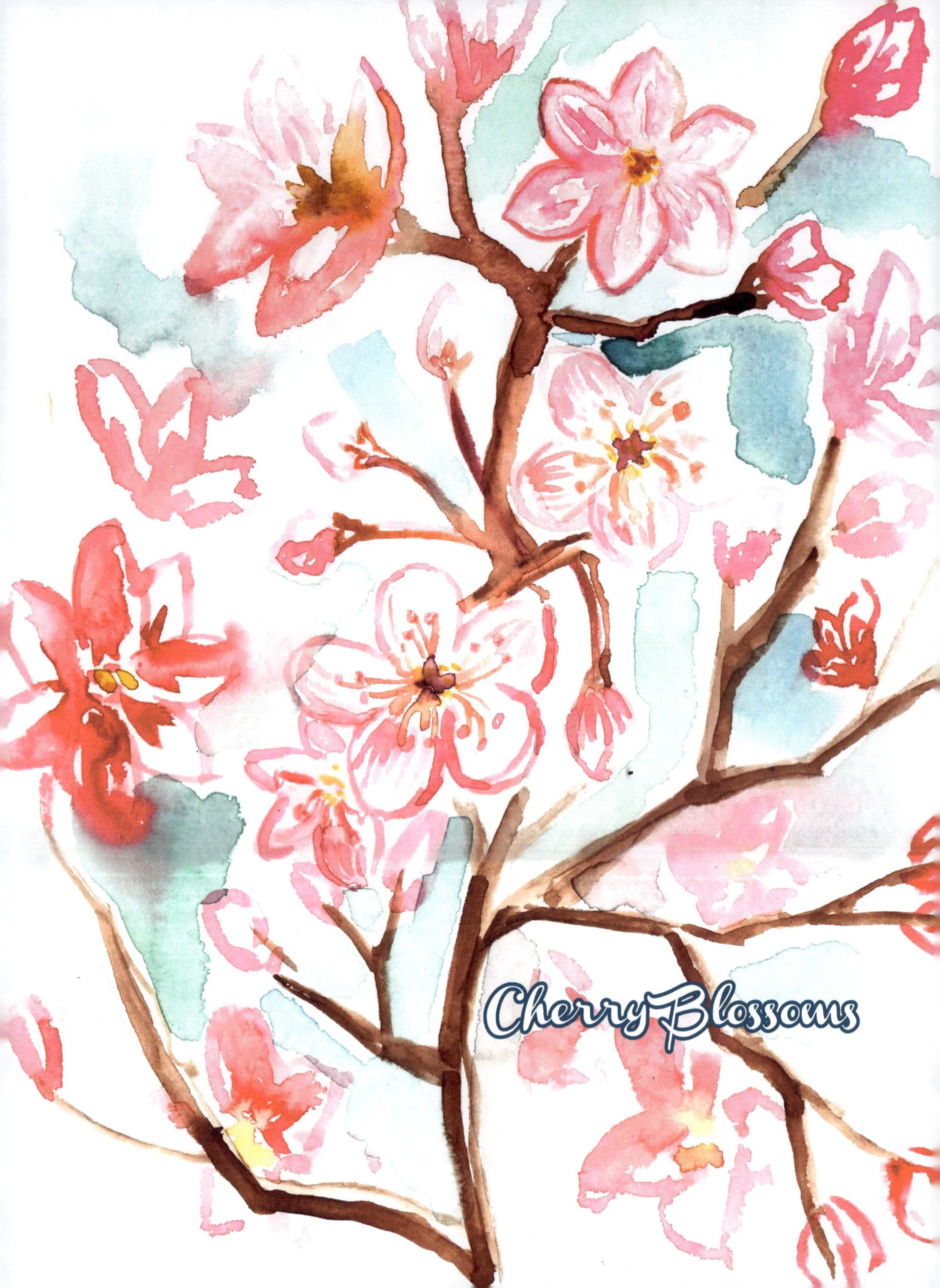

CherryBlossoms

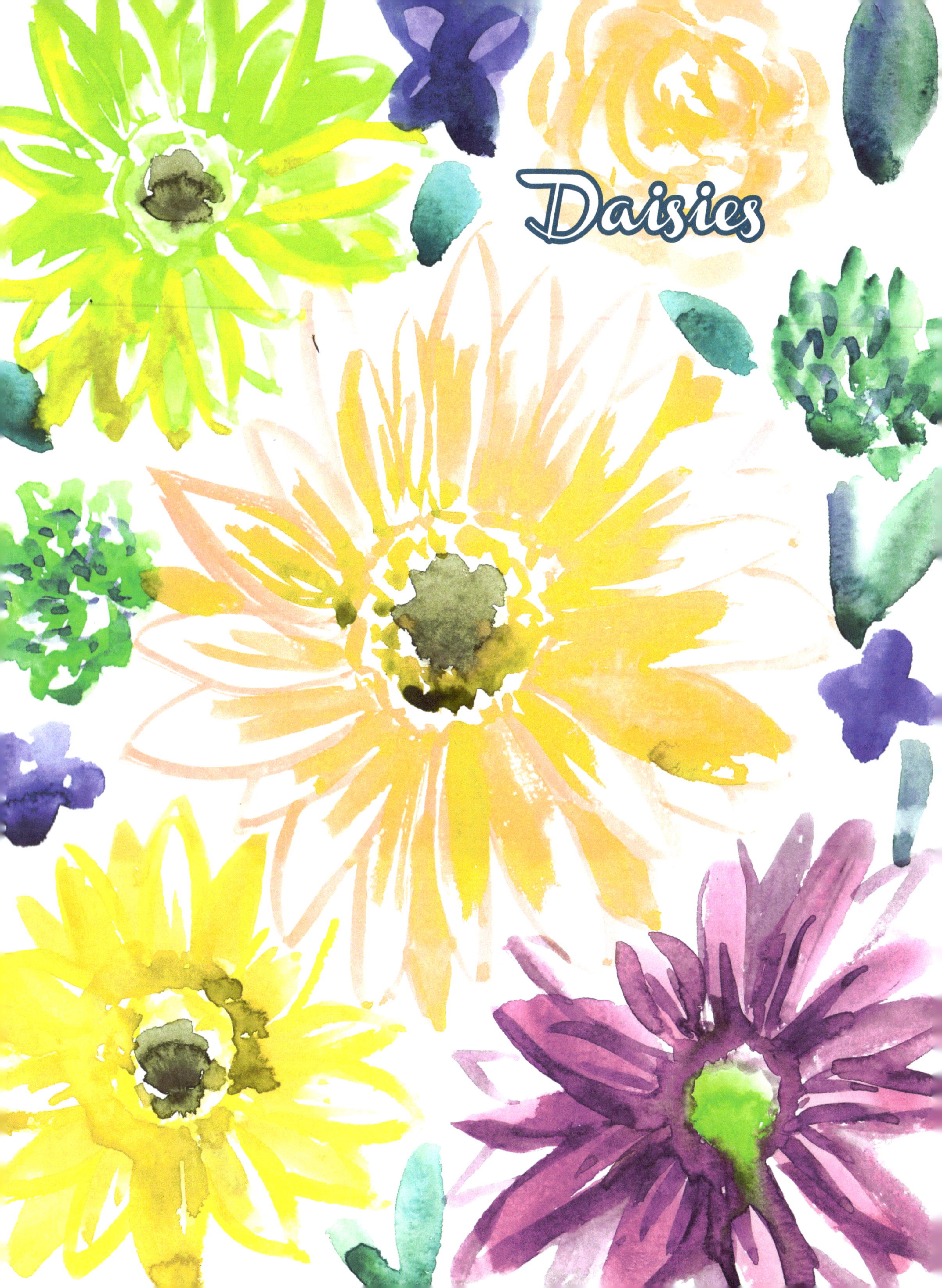
Daisies

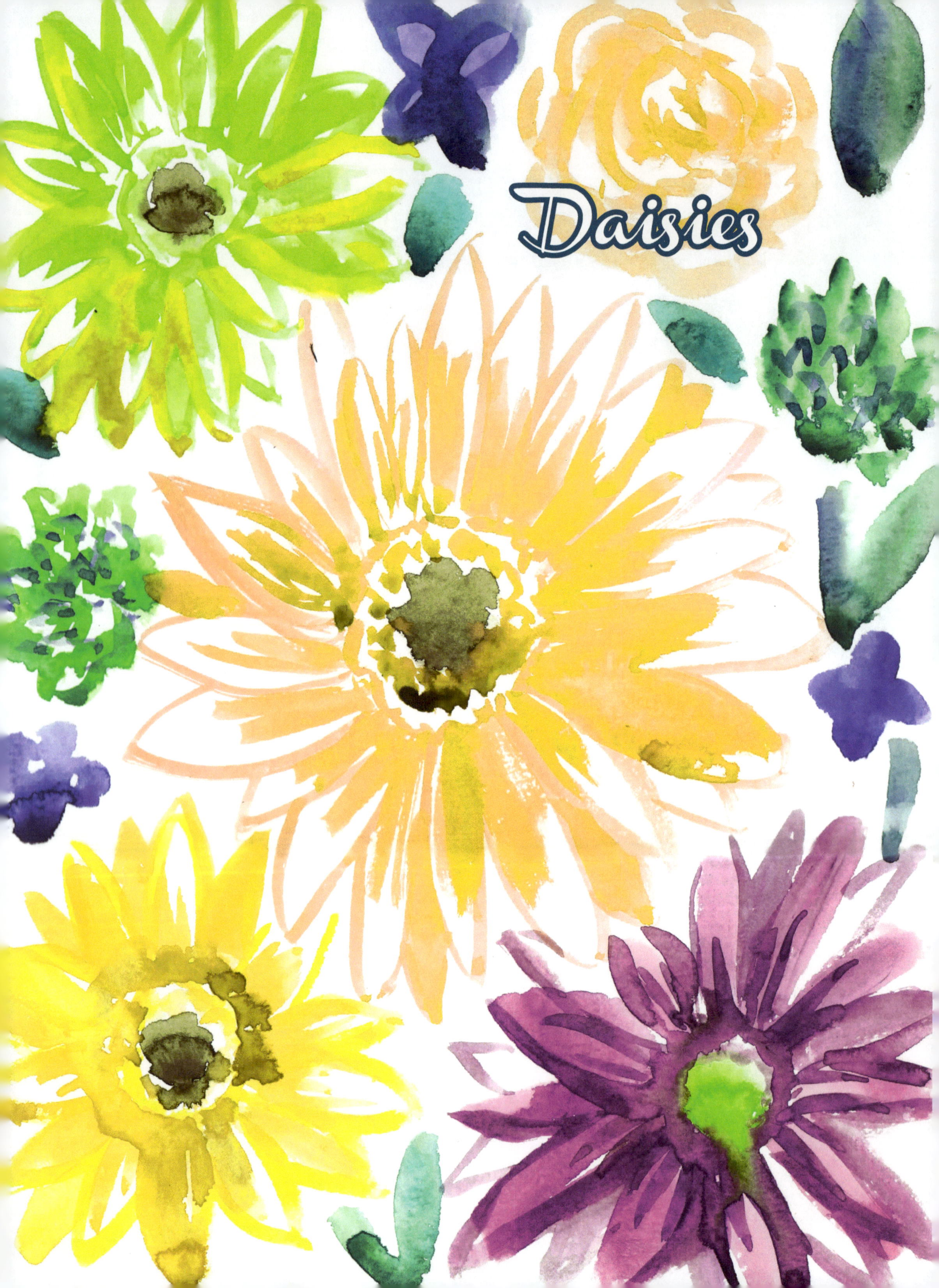
Daisies

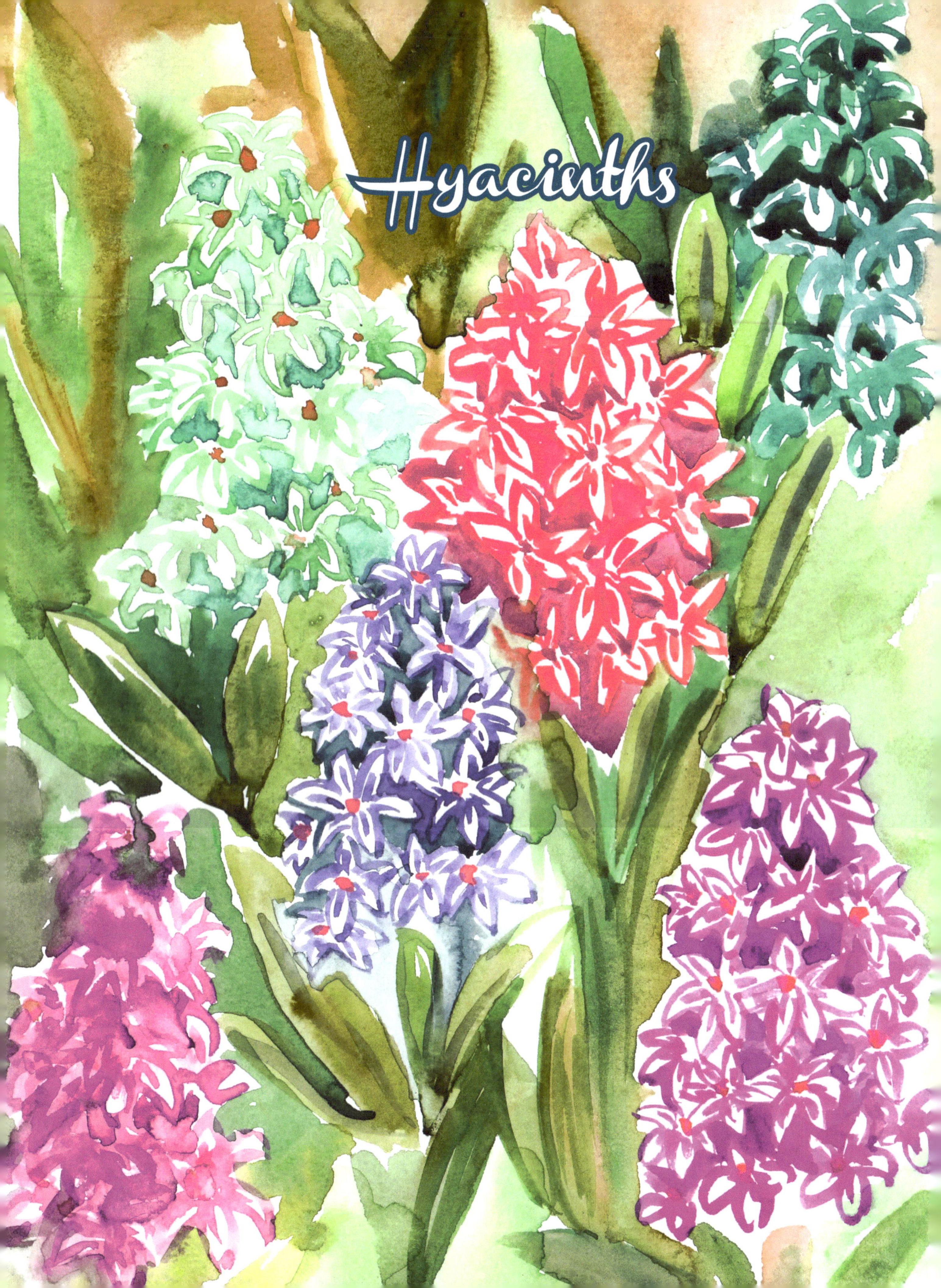
Hyacinths

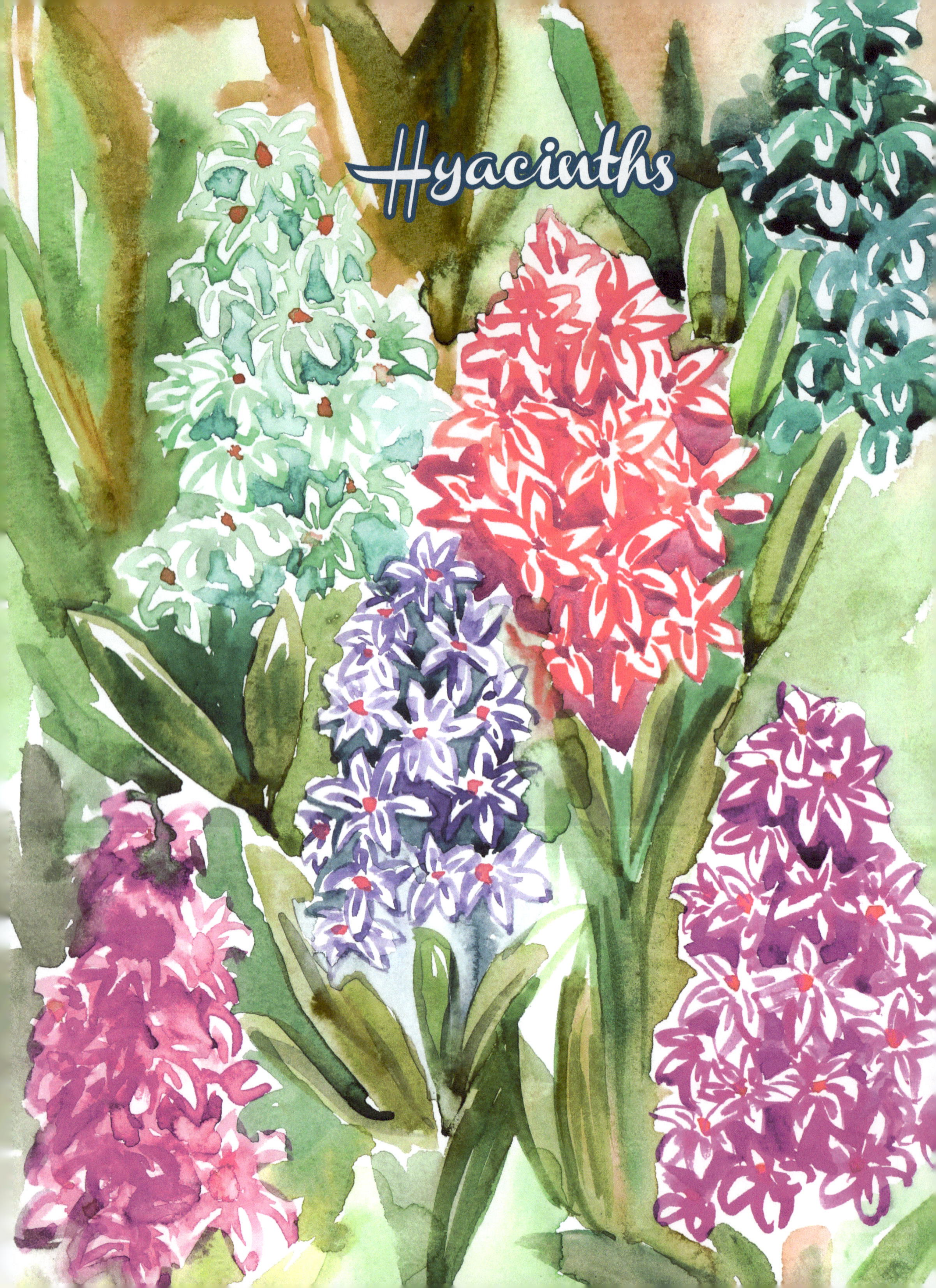

Hyacinths

Tulips

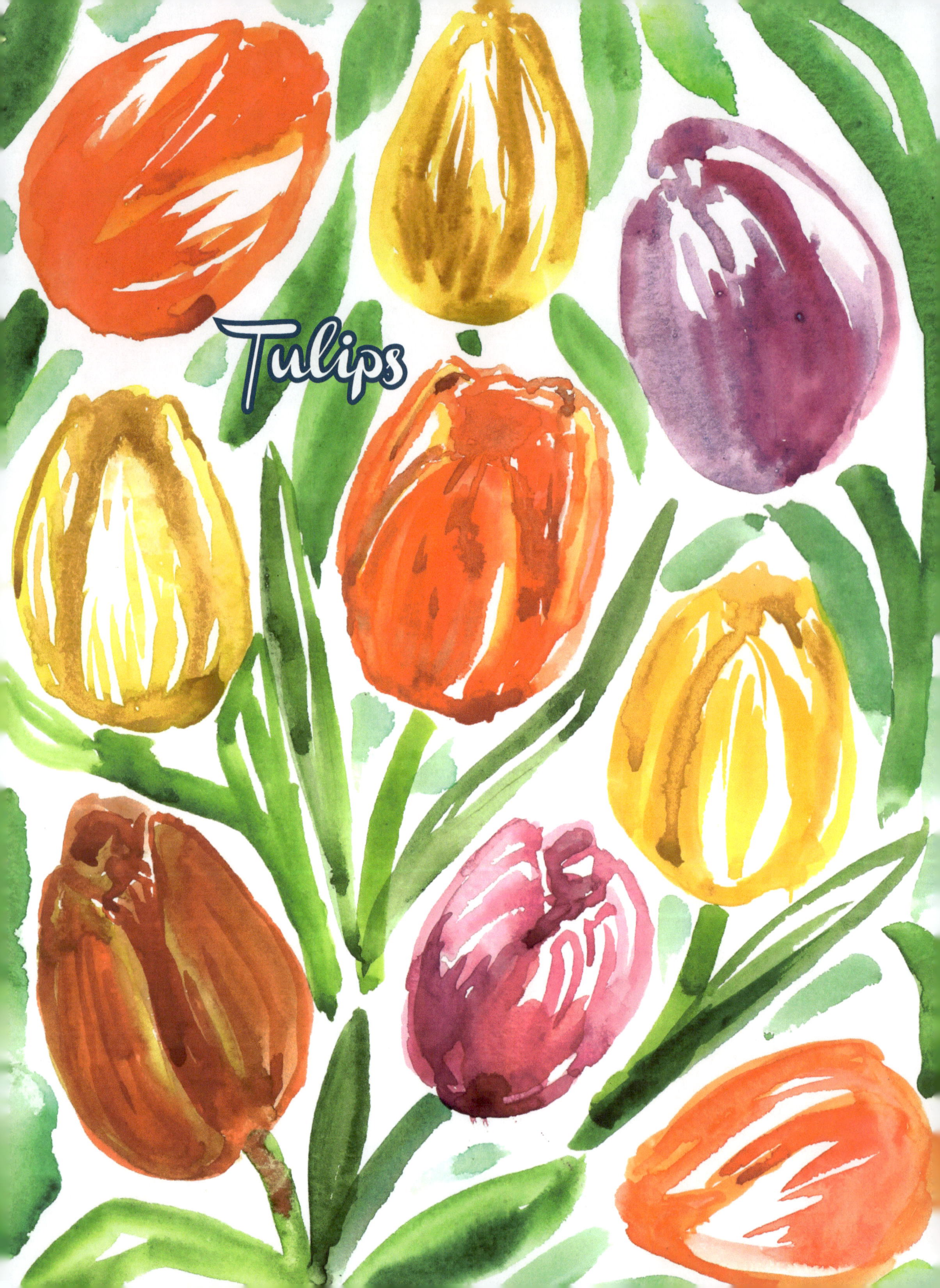
Tulips

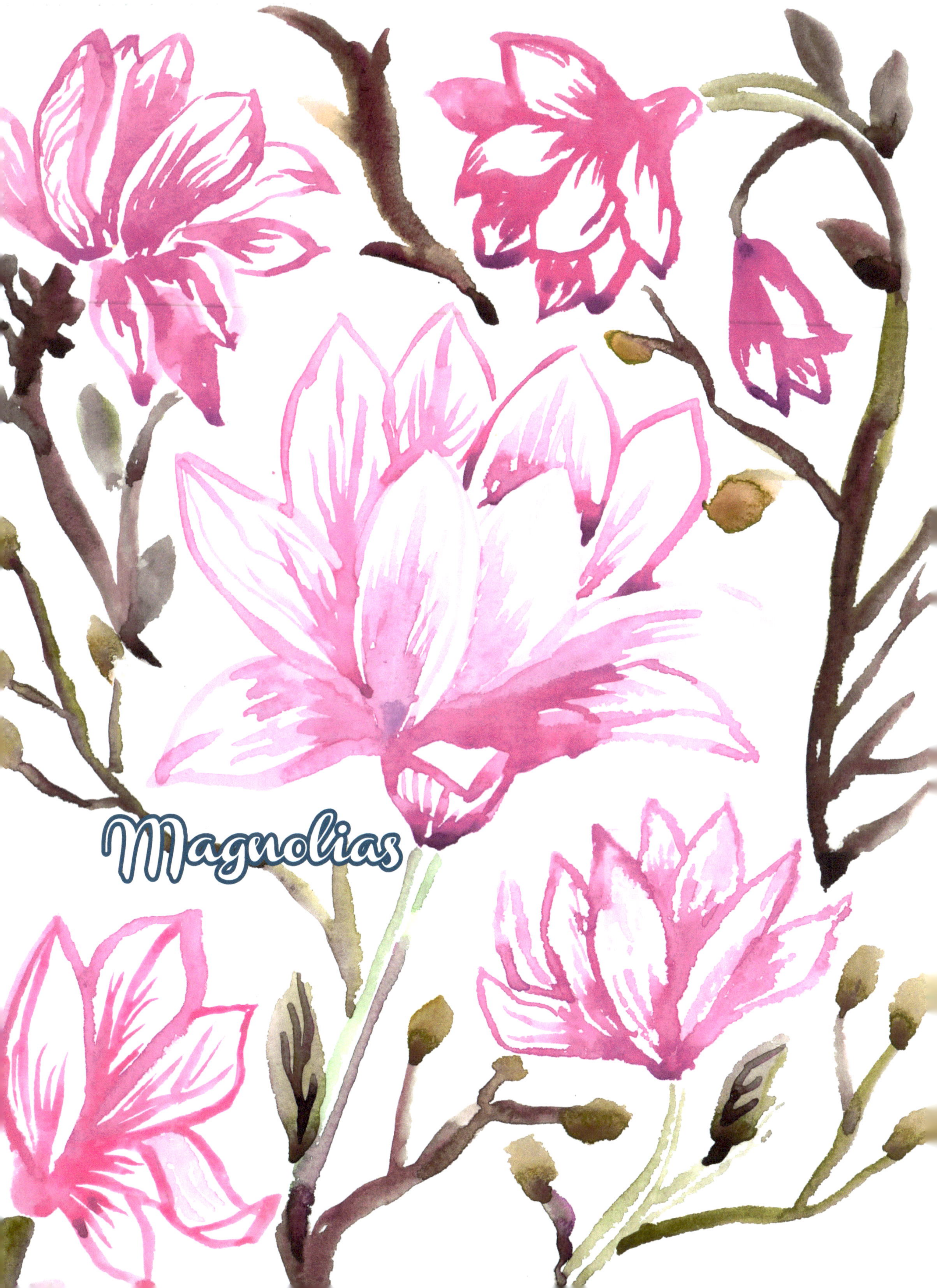
Magnolias

Magnolias

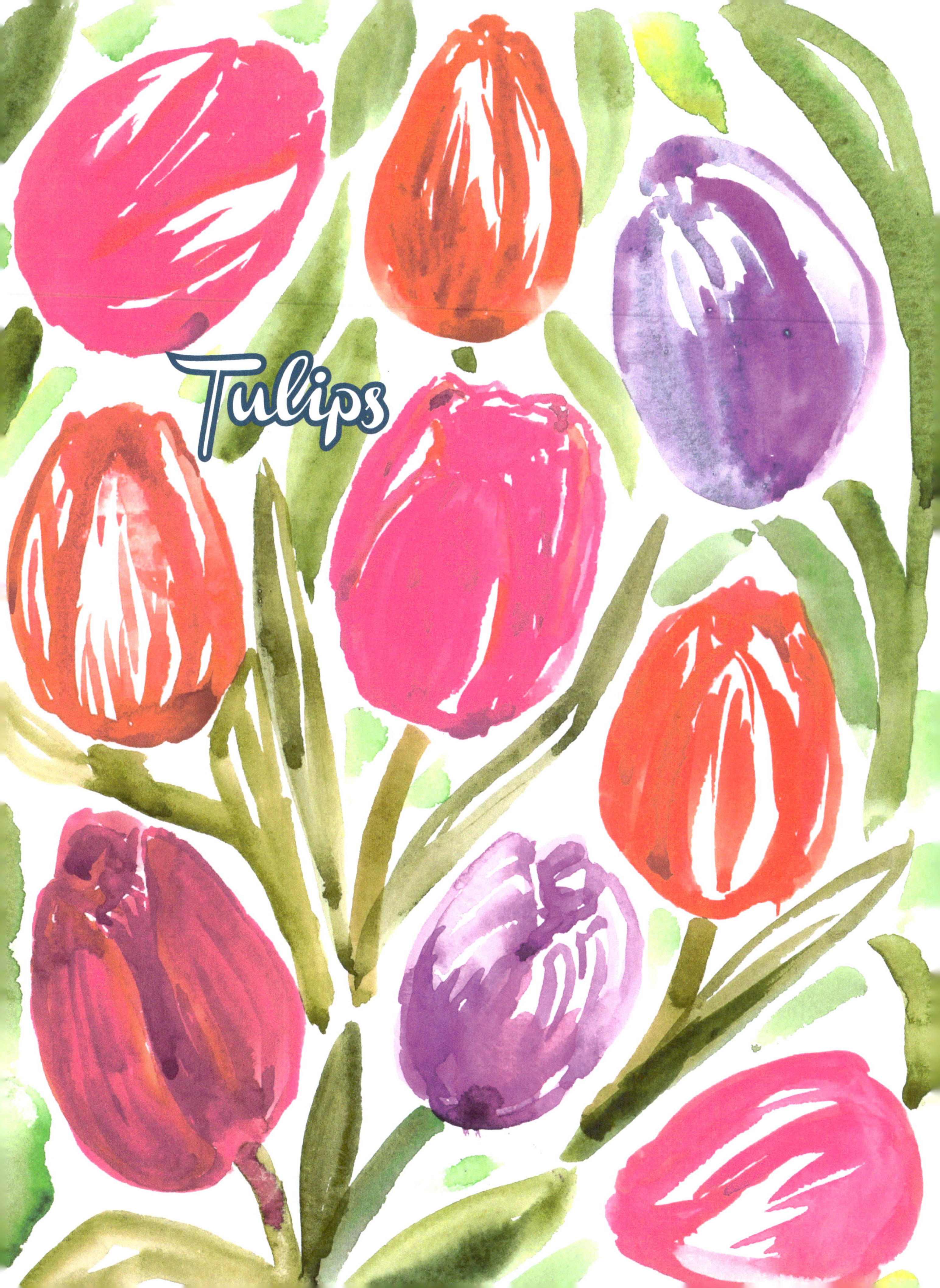

Tulips

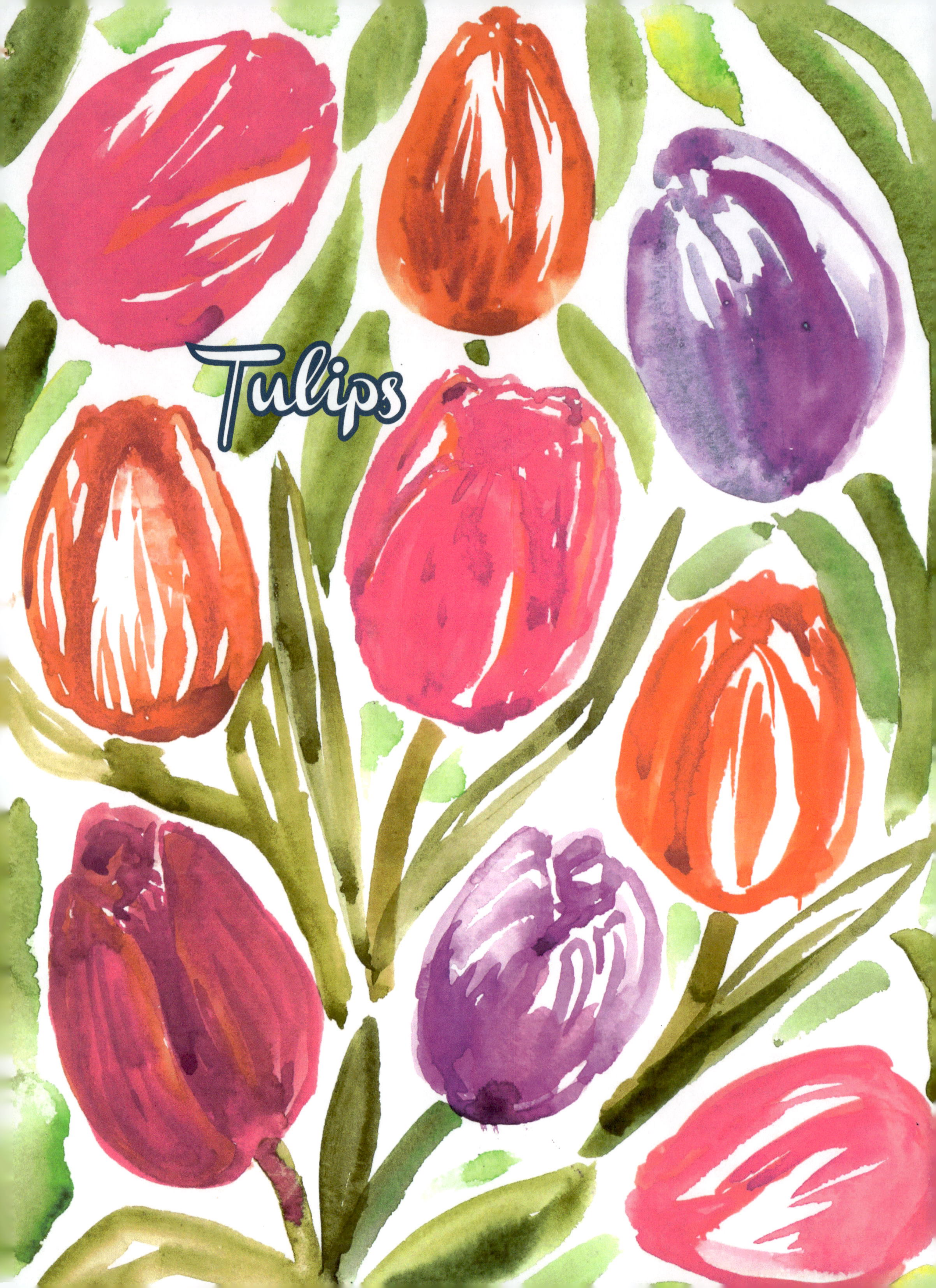
Tulips

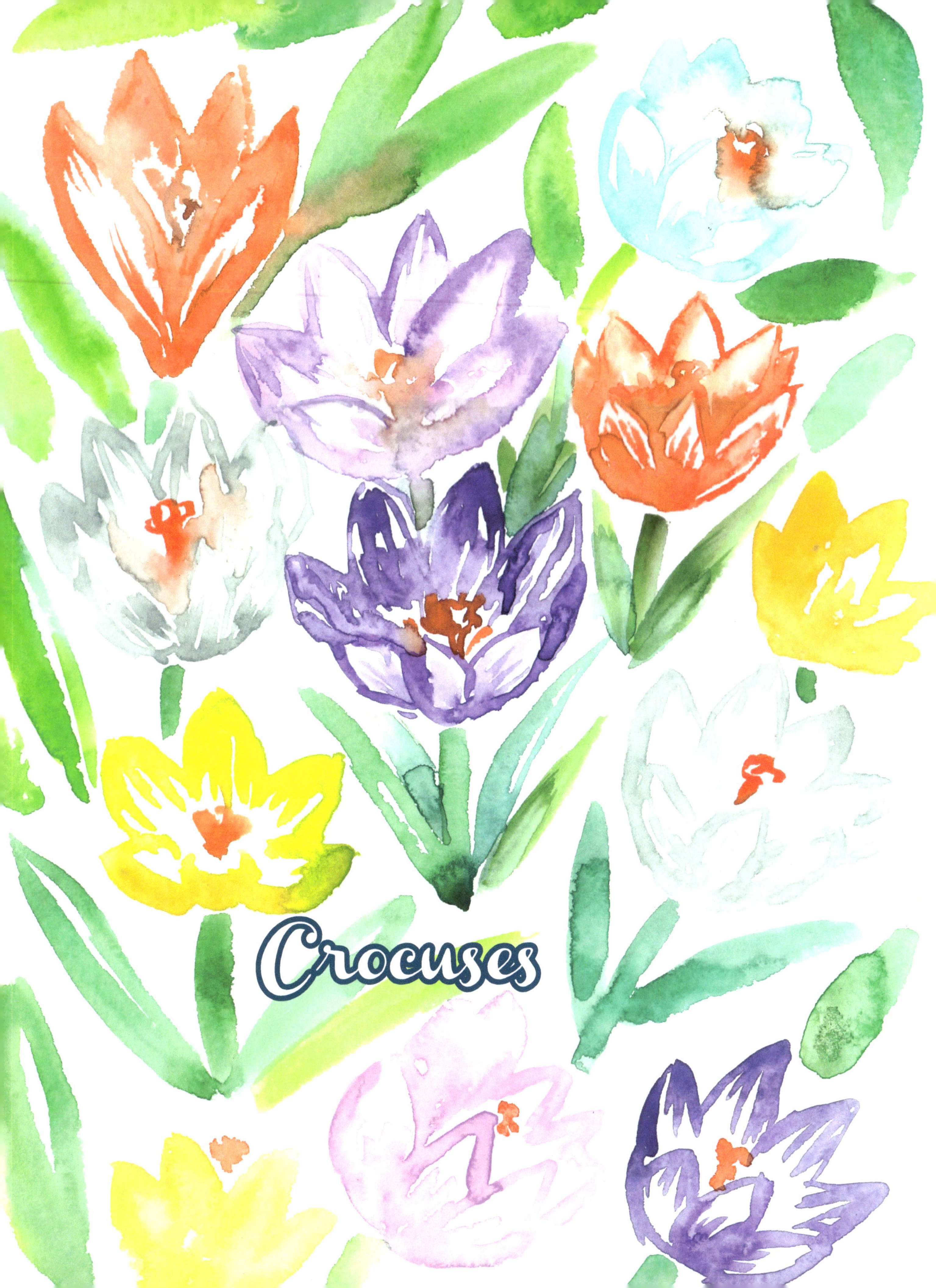
Crocuses

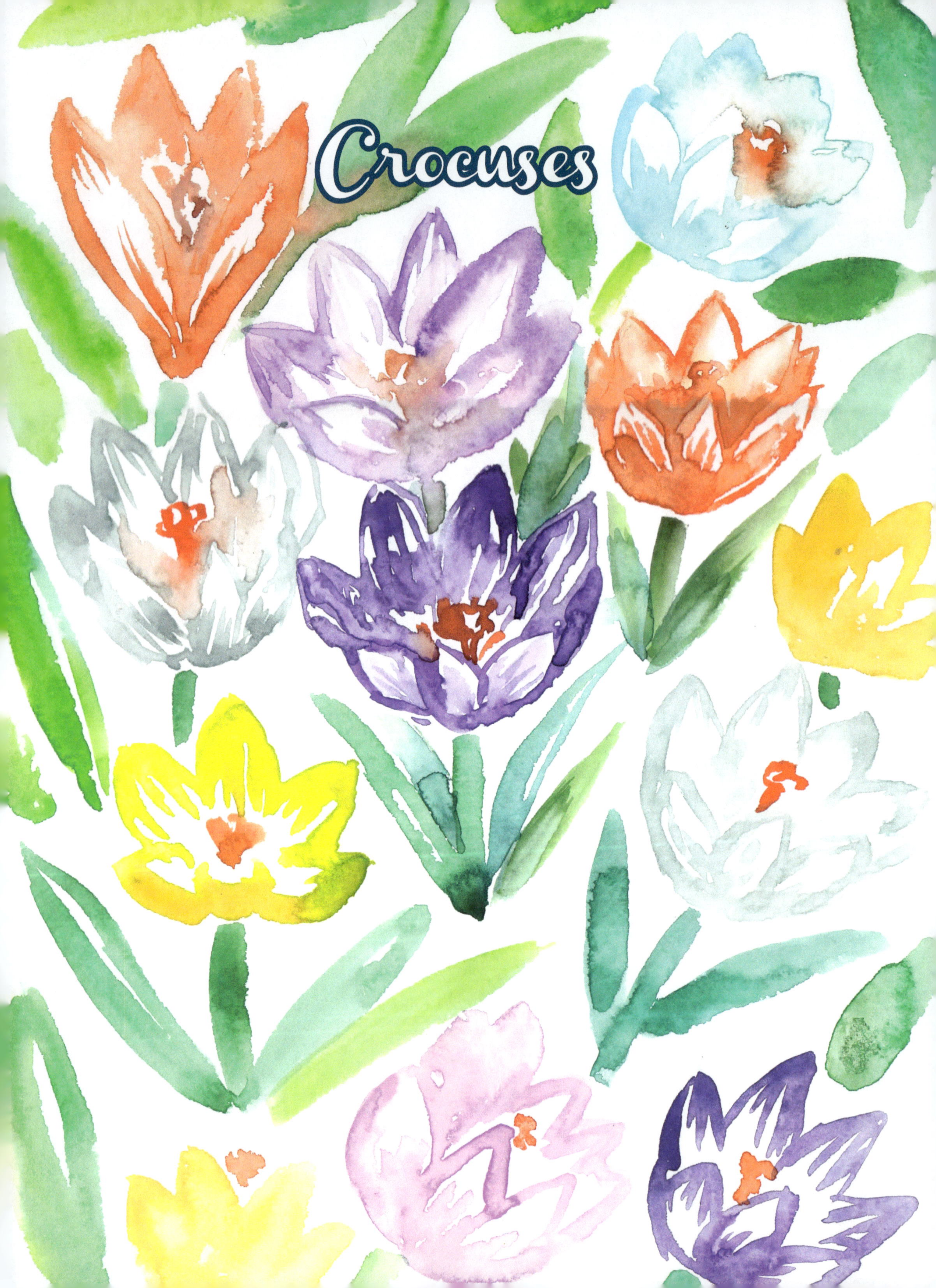
Crocuses

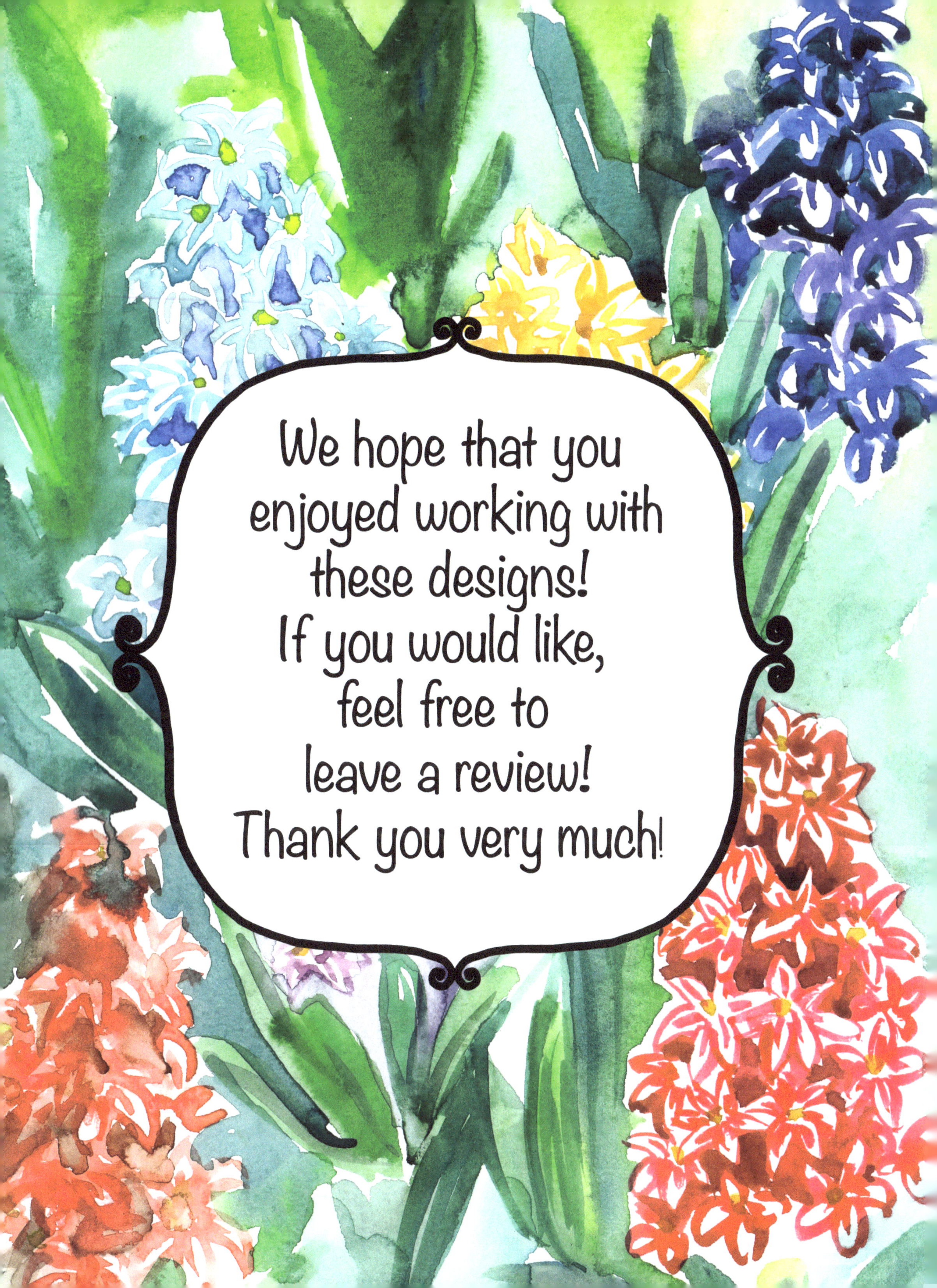
We hope that you
enjoyed working with
these designs!
If you would like,
feel free to
leave a review!
Thank you very much!